SUBSTANCE ABUSE ASSESSMENT, INTERVENTIONS AND TREATMENT



# SUBSTANCE USE AMONG SELECT ETHNICITIES

## ADULTS AND ADOLESCENTS

# Substance Abuse Assessment, Interventions and Treatment

Additional books in this series can be found on Nova's website under the Series tab.

Additional E-books in this series can be found on Nova's website under the E-book tab.

SUBSTANCE ABUSE ASSESSMENT, INTERVENTIONS AND TREATMENT

# SUBSTANCE USE AMONG SELECT ETHNICITIES

## ADULTS AND ADOLESCENTS

RON N. GUROVITZ
EDITOR

NOVINKA
New York

For permission to use material from this book please contact us:
Telephone 631-231-7269; Fax 631-231-8175
Web Site: http://www.novapublishers.com



Additional color graphics may be available in the e-book version of this book.

**Library of Congress Cataloging-in-Publication Data**

ISBN: 978-1-62808-631-7

*Published by Nova Science Publishers, Inc. †New York*

# CONTENTS

# PREFACE

Over the past several decades, the population of the United States has become increasingly diverse. According to the U.S. Census Bureau, about one third of the population belongs to a racial/ethnic minority group; this percentage is projected to increase to 54 percent by 2050. As the country becomes more diverse, it becomes increasingly important to address health and health care disparities related to race/ethnicity, as well as age and gender, socioeconomic status, geography, and disability. The Nation's success in reducing these disparities today, to a large extent, will determine the health of our Nation tomorrow.

One area of concern is assessing substance use and abuse and ensuring access to substance abuse treatment. Substance abuse affects millions of people every year and has untold health, social, and economic costs for individuals, families, and communities. Although it affects people in all racial/ethnic groups, research has shown that there is considerable variation among these groups. Gaining a better under-standing of the behavioral health needs of particular racial/ethnic groups can help inform public health policy, build prevention and treatment programs that target the different needs of these populations, and ultimately ensure that services are available to all individuals who need them.

This book uses data from the National Survey on Drug Use and Health (NSDUH) to examine substance use and treatment need among African-American adults and adolescents; American Indian or Alaska Native adults and adolescents; Hispanic adults and adolescents; and Asian adults and adolescents.

Chapter 1 – Report on Substance Abuse and Mental Health Services Administration, on The NSDUH Report: Substance Use Among Black Adults, February 18, 2010.

Chapter 2 – Report on Substance Abuse and Mental Health Services Administration, on The NSDUH Report: Substance Use Among American Indians or Alaska Native Adults, June 24, 2010.

Chapter 3 – Report on Substance Abuse and Mental Health Services Administration, on The NSDUH Report: Substance Use Among Hispanic Adults, May 27, 2010.

Chapter 4 – Report on Substance Abuse and Mental Health Services Administration, on The NSDUH Report: Substance Use Among Asian Adults, May 20, 2010.

Chapter 5 – Report on Substance Abuse and Mental Health Services Administration, on The NSDUH Report: Substance Use Among Black Adolescents, October 4, 2011.

Chapter 6 – Report on Substance Abuse and Mental Health Services Administration, on The NSDUH Report: Substance Use Among American Indian and Alaska Native Adolescents, October 4, 2011.

Chapter 7 – Report on Substance Abuse and Mental Health Services Administration, on The NSDUH Report: Substance Use Among Hispanic Adolescents, October 4, 2011.

Chapter 8 – Report on Substance Abuse and Mental Health Services Administration, on The NSDUH Report: Substance Use Among Asian Adolescents, October 4, 2011.

In: Substance Use Among Select Ethnicities ISBN: 978-1-62808-631-7
Editor: Ron N. Gurovitz 

*Chapter 1*

# THE NSDUH REPORT: SUBSTANCE USE AMONG BLACK ADULTS*

## *National Survey on Drug Use and Health*

## IN BRIEF

- Rates of past month alcohol use and binge alcohol use were lower among black adults aged 18 or older than the national average for adults (44.3 vs. 55.2 percent and 21.7 vs. 24.5 percent, respectively); the rate of past month illicit drug use, however, was higher among black adults than the national average (9.5 vs. 7.9 percent)
- The rate of need for treatment for an alcohol use problem in the past year among black adults was similar to that of the national average among adults (7.7 and 8.1 percent); however, the rate of need for treatment for an illicit drug use problem was higher among blacks than the national average (4.4 vs. 2.9 percent)
- One in seven (14.2 percent) black adults in need of alcohol treatment in the past year and 24.2 percent of those in need of illicit drug treatment received treatment at a specialty facility; both of these rates were higher than the national averages for adults

* This report (NSDUH 174) was released by the Substance Abuse and Mental Health Services Administration, Office of Applied Studies, February 18, 2010.

Over the past several decades, the population of the United States has become increasingly diverse. According to the U.S. Census Bureau, about one third of the population belongs to a racial/ethnic minority group; this percentage is projected to increase to 54 percent by 2050.[1] As the country becomes more diverse, it becomes increasingly important to address health and health care disparities related to race/ethnicity, as well as age and gender, socioeconomic status, geography, and disability. The Nation's success in reducing these disparities today, to a large extent, will determine the health of our Nation tomorrow.

One area of concern is assessing substance use and abuse and ensuring access to substance abuse treatment. Substance abuse affects millions of people every year and has untold health, social, and economic costs for individuals, families, and communities. Although it affects people in all racial/ethnic groups, research has shown that there is considerable variation among these groups.

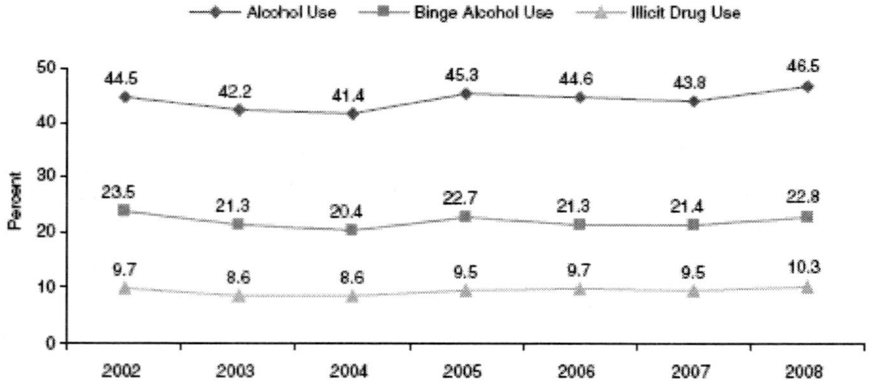


Source: 2002 to 2008 SAMHSA National Surveys on Drug Use and Health (NSDUHs).

Figure 1. Trends in Past Month Substance Use among Blacks Aged 18 or Older: 2002 to 2008.

Gaining a better under-standing of the behavioral health needs of particular racial/ethnic groups can help inform public health policy, build prevention and treatment programs that target the different needs of these populations, and ultimately ensure that services are available to all individuals who need them.

This report uses data from the National Survey on Drug Use and Health (NSDUH) to examine substance use and treatment need among non-Hispanic black or African American adults (hereafter referred to as “black adults”) aged 18 or older.[2] Later reports in this series will examine similar issues among black adolescents and among adults and adolescents in other racial/ethnic groups. According to the U.S. Census Bureau, 37 million people—12.2 percent of the total population in 2008—identify themselves as non-Hispanic blacks of one race.[3]

The first section of this report provides trends in substance use using NSDUH data from 2002 to 2008; the remaining sections present annual averages using combined data from 2004 or 2005 to 2008.

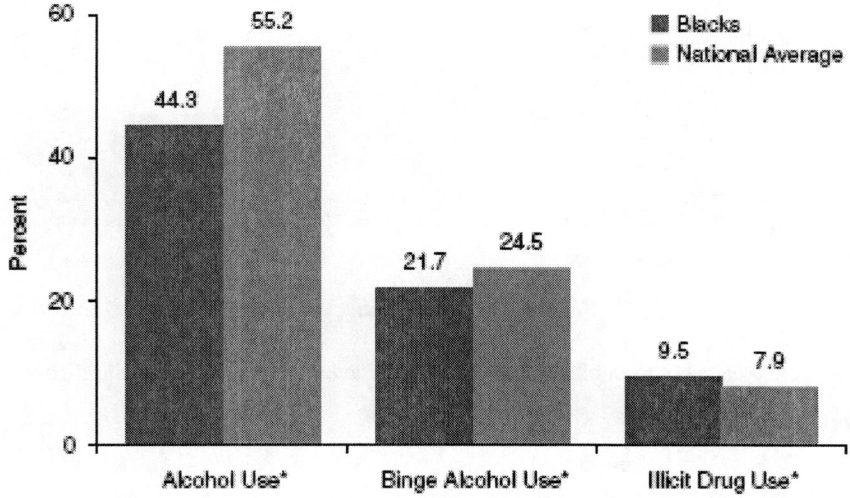


Source: 2004 to 2008 SAMHSA National Surveys on Drug Use and Health (NSDUHs).

* The difference between blacks and the national average is statistically significant at p < .05.

Figure 2. Past Month Substance Use among Blacks Aged 18 or Older Compared with the National Average: 2004 to 2008.

## TRENDS IN SUBSTANCE USE

Past month alcohol use, binge alcohol use, and illicit drug use remained relatively stable among black adults between 2002 and 2008 (Figure1).[4,5]

## PAST MONTH ALCOHOL AND ILLICIT DRUG USE

Combined 2004 to 2008 data indicate that, in the past month, 44.3 percent of black adults used alcohol, 21.7 percent reported binge alcohol use, and 9.5 percent used an illicit drug (Figure 2).

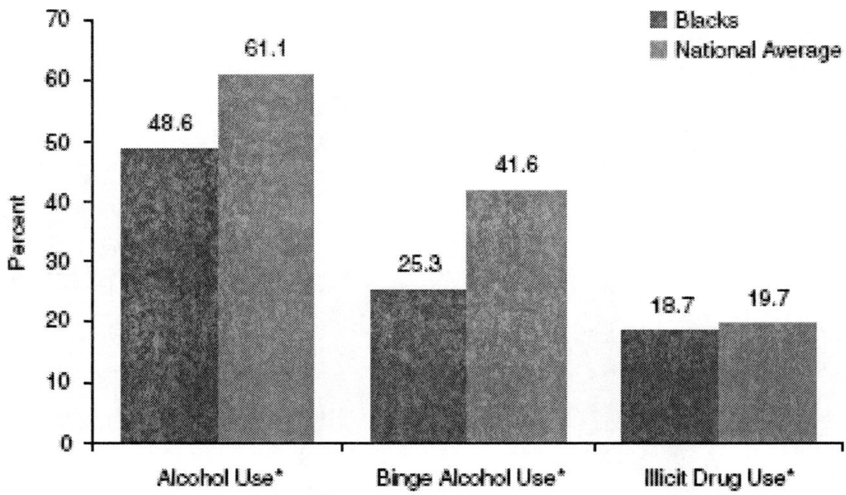


Source: 2004 to 2008 SAMHSA National Surveys on Drug Use and Health (NSDUHs).

* The difference between blacks and the national average is statistically significant at $p < .05$.

Figure 3. Past Month Substance Use among Young Black Adults Aged 18 to 25 Compared with the National Average: 2004 to 2008.

Rates of past month alcohol use and binge alcohol use were lower among black adults than the national averages. The rate of past month illicit drug use among black adults, however, was higher than the national average.

## SUBSTANCE USE AMONG YOUNG ADULTS (AGED 18 TO 25)

Rates of past month and binge alcohol use were considerably lower among young black adults than the national average of young adults (48.6 vs. 61.1 percent and 25.3 vs. 41.6 percent, respectively) (Figure 3). Past month illicit drug use among young black adults was slightly lower than the national average (18.7 vs. 19.7 percent).

## SUBSTANCE USE AMONG OLDER ADULTS (AGED 65 OR OLDER)

Older black adults had a rate of past month alcohol use that was considerably lower than the national average of older adults (20.3 vs. 38.3 percent) (Figure 4). Their rates of binge alcohol use and past month illicit drug use, however, did not differ significantly from the national averages.

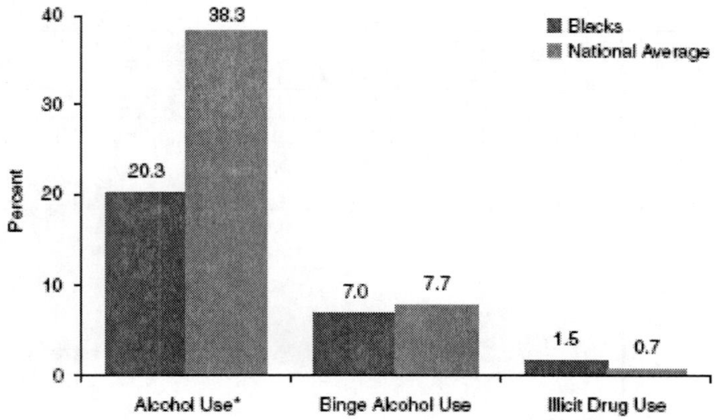


Source: 2004 to 2008 SAMHSA National Surveys on Drug Use and Health (NSDUHs).

* The difference between blacks and the national average is statistically significant at $p < .05$.

Figure 4. Past Month Substance Use among Black Adults Aged 65 or Older Compared with the National Average: 2004 to 2008.

## SUBSTANCE USE AMONG WOMEN

Compared with the national averages, adult black females had lower rates of past month alcohol use and binge alcohol use and a slightly higher rate of past month illicit drug use (Table 1). Patterns varied by age group. Among women aged 18 to 44 who were pregnant at the time of the survey interview, blacks had a higher rate of binge alcohol use than the national average (8.1 vs. 3.6 percent) (Figure 5). As for past month alcohol use and past month illicit drug use, the rates appear to have been higher than the national average of pregnant women, but the differences were not statistically significant.

**Table 1. Substance Use among Black Females Aged 18 or Older compared with the National Average, by Age group: 2004 to 2008**

| Age Group | Alcohol Use: Blacks | Alcohol Use: National Average | Binge Alcohol Use: Blacks | Binge Alcohol Use: National Average | Illicit Drug Use: Blacks | Illicit Drug Use: National Average |
|---|---|---|---|---|---|---|
| Total | 36.6* | 48.5 | 14.4* | 15.9 | 6.2* | 5.7 |
| Aged 18 to 25 | 44.9* | 56.9 | 18.6* | 33.1 | 13.9* | 15.7 |
| Aged 26 to 49 | 43.9* | 53.7 | 17.7* | 18.9 | 6.7 | 6.2 |
| Aged 50 to 64 | 27.3* | 46.7 | 10.4 | 8.9 | 2.5 | 2.8 |
| Aged 65 or Older | 14.4* | 31.5 | 3.5 | 3.7 | 0.7 | 0.5 |

Source: 2004 to 2008 SAMHSA National Surveys on Drug Use and Health (NSDUHs).

* The difference between blacks and the national average is statistically significant at p < .05.

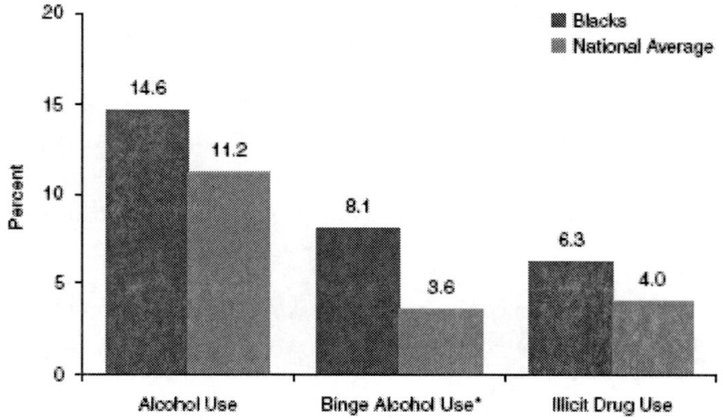


Source: 2004 to 2008 SAMHSA National Surveys on Drug Use and Health (NSDUHs).

* The difference between blacks and the national average is statistically significant at p < .05.

Figure 5. Past Month Substance Use among Black Pregnant Women Aged 18 to 44 Compared with the National Average: 2004 to 2008.

## Substance Use among Men

Compared with the national averages, adult black males had lower rates of past month alcohol use and binge alcohol use and a slightly higher rate of past month illicit drug use (Table 2). Patterns varied by age group.

**Table 2. Substance Use among Black Males Aged 18 or Older compared with the National Average, by Age group: 2004 to 2008**

| Age Group | Alcohol Use: Blacks | Alcohol Use: National Average | Binge Alcohol Use: Blacks | Binge Alcohol Use: National Average | Illicit Drug Use: Blacks | Illicit Drug Use: National Average |
|---|---|---|---|---|---|---|
| Total | 54.0* | 62.3 | 30.8* | 33.8 | 13.7* | 10.2 |
| Aged 18 to 25 | 52.6* | 65.3 | 32.7* | 50.0 | 23.9 | 23.8 |
| Aged 26 to 49 | 61.5* | 67.4 | 35.2* | 39.2 | 14.7* | 11.2 |
| Aged 50 to 64 | 49.7* | 59.3 | 27.9 | 25.0 | 7.1 | 4.9 |
| Aged 65 or Older | 29.8* | 47.4 | 12.5 | 13.2 | 2.8 | 1.0 |

Source: 2004 to 2008 SAMHSA National Surveys on Drug Use and Health (NSDUHs).

* The difference between blacks and the national average is statistically significant at $p < .05$.

## Substance Use among Uninsured Persons

Nearly one fifth of black adults (17.5 percent) were without health insurance, a percentage higher than the national average of 15.0 percent for adults.[6] Uninsured blacks weremore likely than the national average of uninsured adults to have used illicit drugs in the past month (18.2 vs. 15.1 percent) and less likely to have binged on alcohol in the past month (31.0 vs. 33.1 percent); no statistically significant difference was found between these two groups for past month alcohol use (Figure 6).

## Substance Use Among Persons Living in Poverty

Combined 2005 to 2008 data indicate that almost one quarter of black adults (23.3 percent) were living in poverty, a percentage higher than the national average of 11.5 percent.[7]

The rate of past month illicit drug use among blacks living in poverty was slightly higher than the national average of adults living in poverty (12.9 vs. 11.7 percent); rates of past month alcohol use and binge alcohol use, however, did not differ significantly from the national averages (Figure 7).

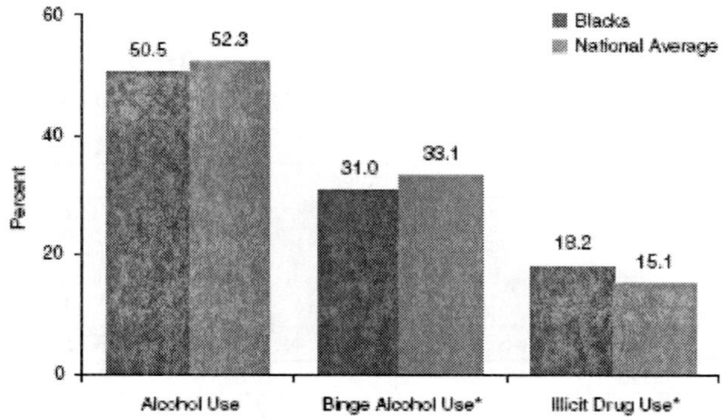


Source: 2004 to 2008 SAMHSA National Surveys on Drug Use and Health (NSDUHs).

* The difference between blacks and the national average is statistically significant at $p < .05$.

Figure 6. Past Month Substance Use among Blacks Aged 18 or Older Who Were Uninsured compared with the National Average: 2004 to 2008.

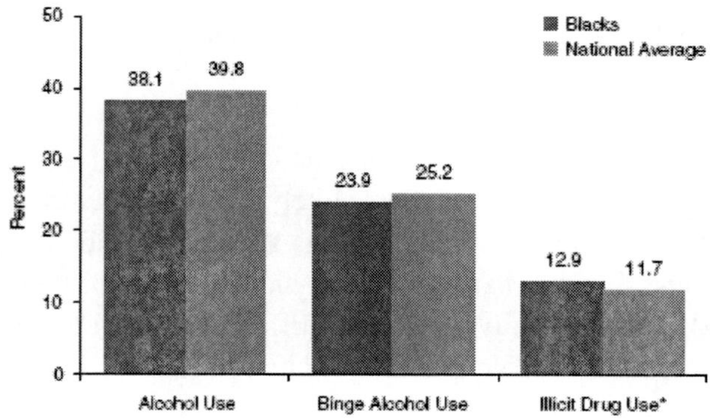


Source: 2005 to 2008 SAMHSA National Surveys on Drug Use and Health (NSDUHs).

The difference between blacks and the national average is statistically significant at $p < .05$.

Figure 7. Past Month Substance Use among Blacks Aged 18 or Older in Poverty compared with the National Average: 2005 to 2008.

## Alcohol Use Treatment

Combined 2004 to 2008 data indicate that an estimated 1.9 million black adults—7.7 percent—were classified as being in need of treatment for an alcohol use problem in the past year.[8] This rate was similar to the national average of 8.1 percent.

One in seven (14.2 percent) black adults in need of alcohol treatment in the past year (274,000 persons) received it at a specialty facility.[9] This rate was higher than the national average of 8.2 percent.

## Illicit Drug Use Treatment

An estimated 1.1 million black adults—or 4.4 percent—were classified as being in need of treatment for an illicit drug use problem in the past year. This rate was higher than the national average of 2.9 percent.

Almost one quarter (24.2 percent) of black adults in need of illicit drug treatment in the past year (267,000 persons) received it at a specialty facility. This rate was higher than the national average of 19.2 percent.

## Discussion

As the Federal Government and States move forward with the interrelated tasks of reducing disparities and reforming health care, it will be vitally important to monitor data on substance use and treatment need among racial/ethnic minorities. The findings in this report highlight variations in substance use and treatment need between black adults and adults in the Nation as a whole and suggest subgroups that may benefit from increased attention from the prevention and treatment systems.

## Note

The National Survey on Drug Use and Health (NSDUH) is an annual survey sponsored by the Substance Abuse and Mental Health Services Administration (SAMHSA). The 2004 to 2008 data used in this report are based on information obtained from 227,791 persons aged 18 or older, including 25,798 blacks or African Americans. The survey collects data by administering questionnaires to a representative sample of the population through face-to-face interviews at their place of residence.

## End Notes

[1] U.S. Census Bureau. (2008, August 14). An older and more diverse Nation by midcentury [U.S. Census Bureau News]. Retrieved January 11, 2010, from http://www.census. gov/Press-Release/www/releases/archives/ population/012496.html.

[2] NSDUH asks a series of questions about race/ ethnicity. First, respondents are asked about their Hispanic origin; then they are asked to identify which racial grouping best describes them: white, black or African American, American Indian or Alaska Native, Native Hawaiians, Other Pacific Islanders, Asian, or other. Respondents may select more than one race. For this report, "black" refers to persons identifying themselves as black or African American only. Persons identifying as black and Hispanic or black and another racial group are not included.

[3] Numbers were calculated from various census tables: U.S. Census Bureau. (2009, December 22). National characteristics. Retrieved January 11, 2010, from http://www.census.gov/ popest/ national/asrh/natasrh.html.

[4] Binge alcohol use is defined as drinking five or more drinks on the same occasion (i.e., at the same time or within a couple of hours of each other) on at least 1 day in the past 30 days.

[5] NSDUH defines illicit drugs as marijuana/ hashish, cocaine (including crack), inhalants, hallucinogens, heroin, or prescription-type drugs used nonmedically. Nonmedical use is defined as the use of prescription-type drugs not prescribed for the respondent by a physician or used only for the experience or feeling they caused. Nonmedical use of any prescription-type pain reliever, sedative, stimulant, or tranquilizer does not include over-the-counter drugs; nonmedical use of stimulants includes methamphetamine use.

[6] A respondent is classified as having health insurance coverage if he or she has private insurance, Medicare, Medicaid/Children's Health Insurance Program (CHIP), Civilian Health and Medical Program of the Uniformed Services (CHAMPUS), TRICARE, Civilian Health and Medical Program of the Department of Veterans Affairs (CHAMPVA), Veterans Affairs (VA), military health care, or any other type of health insurance. All other respondents were classified as without health insurance or uninsured.

[7] NSDUH gathers data on family income, size, and composition (i.e., number of children) and respondent's age. This information is used to determine the respondent's poverty level. The poverty level is calculated as a percentage of the U.S. Census Bureau's poverty threshold by dividing the respondent's reported total family income by the appropriate poverty threshold amount. If a family's total income is less than the family's poverty threshold, then that family and every individual in it is considered to be living in poverty (i.e., less than 100 percent of the U.S. census poverty threshold). Persons aged 18 to 22 living in college dormitories were excluded from this analysis because poverty status is not determined for this group. The poverty variable is available for the years from 2005 to 2008; therefore, information for this estimate is restricted to combined data from these years.

[8] NSDUH classifies persons as needing treatment for alcohol or illicit drug use if they meet the criteria for dependence or abuse or if they received specialty treatment in the past year.

NSDUH defines substance dependence or abuse using criteria specified in the Diagnostic and Statistical Manual of Mental Disorders (DSM-IV), including symptoms such as withdrawal, tolerance, use in dangerous situations, trouble with the law, and interference in major obligations at work, school, or home during the past year. For details, see the following resource: American Psychiatric Association. (1994). Diagnostic and statistical manual of mental disorders (4th ed.). Washington, DC: Author.

[9] Substance use treatment at a specialty facility is defined as treatment received at drug or alcohol rehabilitation facilities (inpatient or outpatient), hospitals (inpatient services only), and mental health centers; it excludes treatment received in an emergency room, private doctor's office, self-help group, prison or jail, or hospital as an outpatient.

In: Substance Use Among Select Ethnicities
Editor: Ron N. Gurovitz
ISBN: 978-1-62808-631-7


*Chapter 2*

# THE NSDUH REPORT: SUBSTANCE USE AMONG AMERICAN INDIANS OR ALASKA NATIVE ADULTS*

## *National Survey on Drug Use and Health*

## IN BRIEF

- The rate of past month alcohol use was lower among American Indian or Alaska Native adults than the national average for adults (43.9 vs. 55.2 percent); the rates of past month binge alcohol use and illicit drug use, however, were higher among American Indian or Alaska Native adults than the national averages (30.6 vs. 24.5 percent and 11.2 vs. 7.9 percent, respectively)
- The percentage of American Indian or Alaska Native adults who needed treatment for an alcohol or illicit drug use problem in the past year was higher than the national average for adults (18.0 vs. 9.6 percent)
- One in eight (12.6 percent) American Indian or Alaska Native adults in need of alcohol or illicit drug use treatment in the past year received treatment at a specialty facility; this rate did not differ significantly from the national average of 10.4 percent

* This report (NSDUH 182) was released by the Substance Abuse and Mental Health Services Administration, Office of Applied Studies, June 24, 2010.

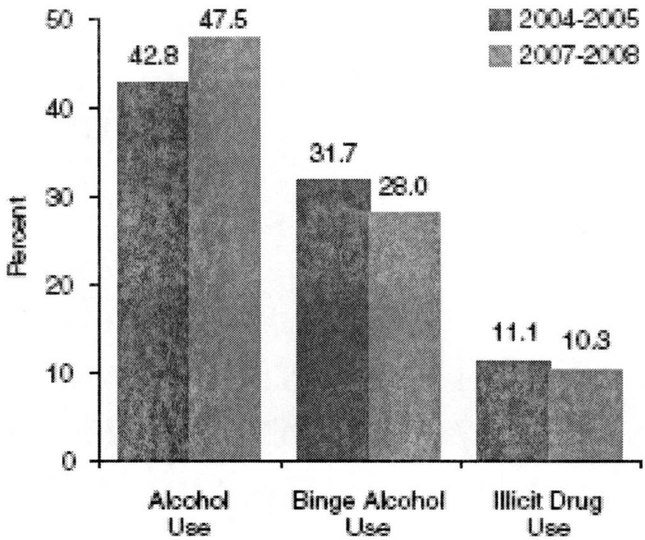


Source: 2004, 2005, 2007, and 2008 SAMHSA National Surveys on Drug Use and Health (NSDUHs).

Figure 1. Past Month Substance Use among American Indians or Alaska Natives Aged 18 or Older: 2004-2005 versus 2007-2008.

Over the past several decades, the population of the United States has become increasingly diverse. According to the U.S. Census Bureau, about one third of the population belongs to a racial/ethnic minority group; this percentage is projected to increase to 54 percent by 2050.[1] As the country becomes more diverse, it becomes increasingly important to address health and health care disparities related to race/ethnicity, as well as age and gender, socioeconomic status, geography, and disability. The Nation's success in reducing these disparities today, to a large extent, will determine the health of our Nation tomorrow.

One area of concern is assessing substance use and abuse and ensuring access to substance abuse treatment. Substance abuse affects millions of people every year and imposes untold health, social, and economic costs on individuals, families, and communities. Although it affects people in all racial/ethnic groups, research has shown that there is considerable variation among these groups.

Gaining a better understanding of the behavioral health needs of particular racial/ethnic groups can help inform public health policy, build prevention and treatment programs that target the different needs of these populations, and expand access to services for individuals who need them.

This report uses data from the National Survey on Drug Use and Health (NSDUH) to examine substance use and treatment need among single-race non-Hispanic American Indian or Alaska Native adults aged 18 or older.[2] Other reports in this series will examine similar issues among American Indian or Alaska Native adolescents and among adults and adolescents in other racial/ethnic groups. According to the U.S. Census Bureau, 2 million people—1.0 percent of the total population in 2008—identify themselves as non-Hispanic American Indian or Alaska Native adults of one race.[3] This report is based on NSDUH data from 2004 to 2008.

## Demographic and Socioeconomic Characteristics

Combined 2004 to 2008 NSDUH data indicate that American Indian or Alaska Native adults were somewhat younger than the national average for adults, a pattern that was more pronounced for women than men (data not shown). For example, 17.8 percent of American Indian or Alaska Native adult females were aged 18 to 25 compared with the national average of 14.2 percent for adult females. Among adult males, the percentage aged 18 to 25 was 16.0 percent for American Indians or Alaska Natives and 15.5 percent overall. Compared with the national average, American Indian or Alaska Native adults were more likely to live in non-metropolitan counties (47.9 vs. 16.8 percent). Nearly one sixth of American Indian or Alaska Native adults (15.8 percent) were without health insurance, a percentage similar to the national average of 15.0 percent for adults.[4]

Combined 2005 to 2008 data indicate that, compared with the national average, American Indian or Alaska Native adults were more likely to be living in poverty (27.6 vs. 11.5 percent).[5]

## Trends in Substance Use

Among American Indian or Alaska Native adults, rates of past month alcohol use, binge alcohol use, and illicit drug use in combined 2007 and 2008 were not significantly different from rates in combined 2004 and 2005 (Figure 1).[6,7]

## PAST MONTH ALCOHOL AND ILLICIT DRUG USE

Combined 2004 to 2008 data indicate that, in the past month, 43.9 percent of American Indian or Alaska Native adults used alcohol, 30.6 percent reported binge alcohol use, and 11.2 percent used an illicit drug (Figure 2).

The rate of past month alcohol use was lower among American Indian or Alaska Native adults than the national average. The rates of past month binge alcohol use and illicit drug use among American Indian or Alaska Native adults, however, were higher than the national averages.

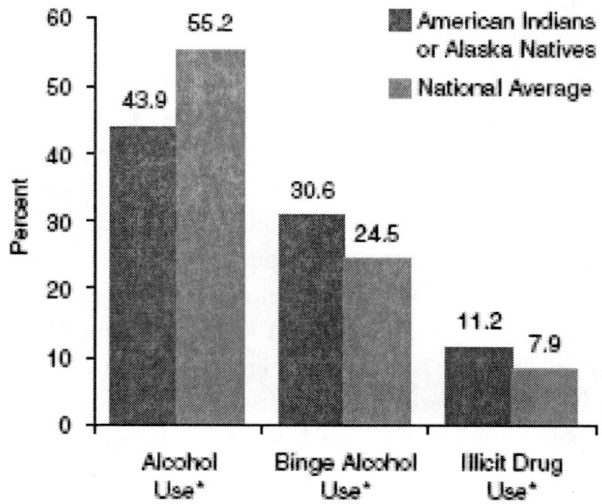


Source: 2004 to 2008 SAMHSA National Surveys on Drug Use and Health (NSDUHs).

* The difference between American Indians or Alaska Natives and the national average is statistically significant at the .05 level.

Figure 2. Past Month Substance Use among American Indians or Alaska Natives Aged 18 or Older Compared with the National Average: 2004 to 2008.

## SUBSTANCE USE, BY AGE GROUP

The rate of past month alcohol use was lower among American Indian or Alaska Native adults than among adults in the general population in each of the three age groups presented in Table 1. Past month binge alcohol use among

American Indians or Alaska Natives aged 26 to 49 was higher than the national average for this age group (39.4 vs. 28.9 percent).

Past month illicit drug use among American Indians or Alaska Natives aged 18 to 25 was higher than the national average for this age group (25.4 vs. 19.7 percent).

## SUBSTANCE USE AMONG WOMEN

Compared with the national averages for adult women, adult American Indian or Alaska Native females had a lower rate of past month alcohol use but higher rates of past month binge alcohol use and illicit drug use (Figure 3).

## SUBSTANCE USE AMONG MEN

Compared with the national averages for adult men, adult American Indian or Alaska Native males had a lower rate of past month alcohol use but a higher rate of past month illicit drug use (Figure 3).

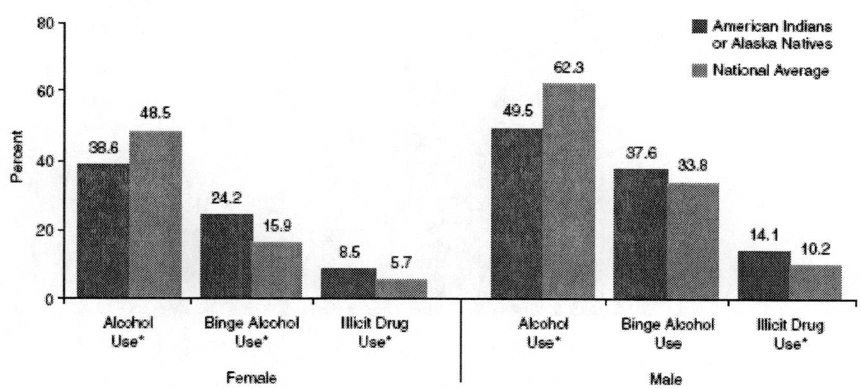


Source: 2004 to 2008 SAMHSA National Surveys on Drug Use and Health (NSDUHs).

* The difference between American Indians or Alaska Natives and the national average is statistically significant at the .05 level.

Figure 3. Past Month Substance Use among American Indians or Alaska Natives Aged 18 or Older Compared with the National Average, by Gender: 2004 to 2008.

**Table 1. Past Month Substance Use among American Indians or Alaska Natives Aged 18 or Older Compared with the National Average, by Age Group: Percentages, 2004 to 2008**

| | Alcohol Use | | Binge Alcohol Use | | Illicit Drug Use | |
|---|---|---|---|---|---|---|
| Age Group | American Indians or Alaska Natives | National Average | American Indians or Alaska Natives | National Average | American Indians or Alaska Natives | National Average |
| Aged 18 to 25 | | | | | | |
| Aged 26 to 49 | 52.0* | 61.1 | 41.2 | 41.6 | 25.4* | 19.7 |
| Aged 50 or | 51.3* | 60.5 | 39.4* | 28.9 | 11.7 | 8.7 |
| Older | 31.0* | 46.9 | 14.9 | 13.0 | 4.1 | 2.5 |

Source: 2004 to 2008 SAMHSA National Surveys on Drug Use and Health (NSDUHs).

* The difference between American Indians or Alaska Natives and the national average is statistically significant at the .05 level.

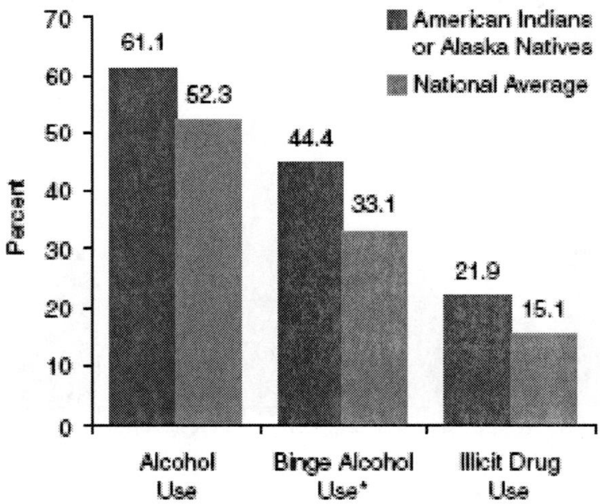


Source: 2004 to 2008 SAMHSA National Surveys on Drug Use and Health (NSDUHs).

* The difference between American Indians or Alaska Natives and the national average is statistically significant at the .05 level.

Figure 4. Past Month Substance Use among American Indians or Alaska Natives Aged 18 or Older Who Were Uninsured Compared with the National Average: 2004 to 2008.

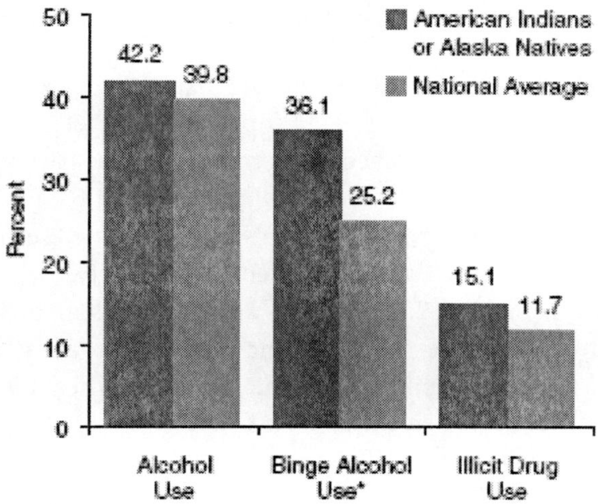


Source: 2005 to 2008 SAMHSA National Surveys on Drug Use and Health (NSDUHs).

* The difference between American Indians or Alaska Natives and the national average is statistically significant at the .05 level.

Figure 5. Past Month Substance Use among American Indians or Alaska Natives Aged 18 or Older Living in Poverty Compared with the National Average: 2005 to 2008.

## SUBSTANCE USE AMONG UNINSURED PERSONS

Uninsured American Indian or Alaska Native adults were more likely than uninsured adults in the general population to have binged on alcohol in the past month (44.4 vs. 33.1 percent); differences between these two groups for past month alcohol use or illicit drug use were not statistically significant (Figure 4).

## SUBSTANCE USE AMONG PERSONS LIVING IN POVERTY

The rate of past month binge alcohol use among American Indian or Alaska Native adults living in poverty was higher than among adults in the general population living in poverty (36.1 vs. 25.2 percent); the rates of past month alcohol use and illicit drug use, however, did not differ significantly from the national averages for adults living in poverty (Figure 5).

## Substance Use Treatment

Combined 2004 to 2008 data indicate that 18.0 percent of American Indian or Alaska Native adults (194,000 people) were classified as being in need of treatment for a substance use problem in the past year, with 14.8 percent in need of treatment for an alcohol problem and 6.0 percent in need of treatment for an illicit drug use problem[8] These rates were higher than the national averages of 9.6, 8.1, and 2.9 percent, respectively.

About one in eight (12.6 percent) American Indian or Alaska Native adults in need of substance use treatment in the past year (24,000 persons) received it at a specialty facility.[9] This rate is not significantly different from the national average (10.4 percent).

## Discussion

As the Federal Government and States move forward with the interrelated tasks of reducing disparities and reforming health care, it will be important to monitor data on substance use and treatment need among racial/ethnic minorities.

The findings in this report highlight variations in substance use and treatment need between American Indian or Alaska Native adults and adults in the Nation as a whole and suggest subgroups that may benefit from increased attention from the prevention and treatment systems.

## Note

The National Survey on Drug Use and Health (NSDUH) is an annual survey sponsored by the Substance Abuse and Mental Health Services Administration (SAMHSA). The 2004 to 2008 data used in this report are based on information obtained from 227,791 persons aged 18 or older, including 2,879 American Indians or Alaska Natives. The survey collects data by administering questionnaires to a representative sample of the population through face-to-face interviews at their place of residence.

# End Notes

[1] U.S. Census Bureau. (2008, August 14). An older and more diverse Nation by midcentury [U.S. Census Bureau News]. Retrieved May 13, 2010, from http://www.census.gov/ newsroom/ releases/archives/population/cb08-123.html.

[2] NSDUH asks a series of questions about race/ethnicity. First, respondents are asked about their Hispanic origin; then they are asked to identify which racial grouping best describes them: white, black or African American, American Indian or Alaska Native, Native Hawaiian, Other Pacific Islander, Asian, or other. Respondents may select more than one race. For this report, American Indian or Alaska Native refers to persons identifying themselves as American Indian or Alaska Native only. Persons identifying as both American Indian or Alaska Native and Hispanic or as both American Indian or Alaska Native and another racial group are not included.

[3] Numbers were calculated from various census tables: U.S. Census Bureau. (2009, December 22). National characteristics. Retrieved May 13, 2010, from http://www.census.gov/ popest/national/asrh/natasrh.html.

[4] A respondent is classified as having health insurance coverage if he or she has private insurance, Medicare, Medicaid/Children's Health Insurance Program (CHIP), Civilian Health and Medical Program of the Uniformed Services (CHAMPUS), TRICARE, Civilian Health and Medical Program of the Department of Veterans Affairs (CHAMPVA), Veterans Affairs (VA), military health care, or any other type of health insurance. All other respondents were classified as without health insurance or uninsured.

[5] NSDUH gathers data on family income, size, and composition (i.e., number of children) and respondent's age. This information is used to determine the respondent's poverty level. The poverty level is calculated as a percentage of the U.S. Census Bureau's poverty threshold by dividing the respondent's reported total family income by the appropriate poverty threshold amount. If a family's total income is less than the family's poverty threshold, then that family and every individual in it is considered to be living in poverty (i.e., less than 100 percent of the U.S. census poverty threshold). Persons aged 18 to 22 living in college dormitories were excluded from this analysis because poverty status is not determined for this group. The poverty variable is available for the years from 2005 to 2008; therefore, information for this estimate is restricted to combined data from these years.

[6] Binge alcohol use is defined as drinking five or more drinks on the same occasion (i.e., at the same time or within a couple of hours of each other) on at least 1 day in the past 30 days.

[7] NSDUH defines illicit drugs as marijuana/hashish, cocaine (including crack), inhalants, hallucinogens, heroin, or prescription-type drugs used nonmedically. Nonmedical use is defined as the use of prescription-type drugs not prescribed for the respondent by a physician or used only for the experience or feeling they caused. Nonmedical use of any prescription-type pain reliever, sedative, stimulant, or tranquilizer does not include over-the-counter drugs; nonmedical use of stimulants includes methamphetamine use.

[8] NSDUH classifies persons as needing treatment for alcohol or illicit drug use if they meet the criteria for dependence or abuse or if they received specialty treatment in the past year. NSDUH defines substance dependence or abuse using criteria specified in the Diagnostic and Statistical Manual of Mental Disorders (DSM-IV), including symptoms such as withdrawal, tolerance, use in dangerous situations, trouble with the law, and interference in major obligations at work, school, or home during the past year. For details, see the following resource: American Psychiatric Association. (1994). Diagnostic and statistical manual of mental disorders (4th ed.). Washington, DC: Author.

[9] Substance use treatment at a specialty facility is defined as treatment received at drug or alcohol rehabilitation facilities (inpatient or outpatient), hospitals (inpatient services only), and mental health centers; it excludes treatment received in an emergency room, private doctor's office, self-help group, prison or jail, or hospital as an outpatient.

In: Substance Use Among Select Ethnicities ISBN: 978-1-62808-631-7
Editor: Ron N. Gurovitz 

*Chapter 3*

# THE NSDUH REPORT: SUBSTANCE USE AMONG HISPANIC ADULTS*

## *National Survey on Drug Use and Health*

## IN BRIEF

- Rates of past month alcohol use and illicit drug use were lower among Hispanic adults than the national averages for adults (46.1 vs. 55.2 percent and 6.6 vs. 7.9 percent, respectively); however, past month binge alcohol use was higher among Hispanics than the national average (26.3 vs. 24.5 percent)
- Among Hispanic adults, substance use varied greatly by subgroup; past month illicit drug use, for example, ranged from a high of 13.1 percent among adults of Spanish origin (from Spain) to a low of 3.9 percent among those of Dominican origin
- Hispanic adults who were born in the United States had higher rates of past month substance use than Hispanic adults who were not born in the United States, regardless of age
- Among Hispanics who needed treatment for an alcohol or illicit drug problem, the percentage who received such treatment did not differ significantly from the national average

---

* This report (NSDUH 184) was released by the Substance Abuse and Mental Health Services Administration, Office of Applied Studies, May 27, 2010.

Over the past several decades, the population of the United States has become increasingly diverse. According to the U.S. Census Bureau, about one third of the population belongs to a racial/ethnic minority group; this percentage is projected to increase to 54 percent by 2050.[1] As the country becomes more diverse, it becomes increasingly important to address health and health care disparities related to race/ethnicity, as well as age and gender, socioeconomic status, geography, and disability. The Nation's success in reducing these disparities today, to a large extent, will determine the health of our Nation tomorrow.

One area of concern is assessing substance use and abuse and ensuring access to substance abuse treatment. Substance abuse affects millions of people every year and imposes untold health, social, and economic costs on individuals, families, and communities. Although it affects people in all racial/ethnic groups, research has shown that there is considerable variation among these groups. Gaining a better understanding of the behavioral health needs of particular racial/ethnic groups can help inform public health policy, build prevention and treatment programs that target the different needs of these populations, and ultimately expand access to services for individuals who need them.

This report uses data from the National Survey on Drug Use and Health (NSDUH) to examine substance use and treatment need among Hispanic adults aged 18 or older.[2] Other reports in this series will examine similar issues among Hispanic adolescents and among adults and adolescents in other racial/ethnic groups. According to the U.S. Census Bureau, 47 million people—15.4 percent of the total U.S. resident population in 2008—identify themselves as Hispanic.[3] This report is based on NSDUH data from 2004 to 2008.

## Demographic Characteristics

Combined 2004 to 2008 data indicate that more than three fifths of Hispanic adults (62.3 percent) were of Mexican origin, 14.1 percent were of Central or South American origin, 10.2 percent were of Puerto Rican origin, 4.7 percent were of Spanish origin (from Spain), 4.3 percent were of Cuban origin, 2.5 percent were of Dominican origin, 1.7 percent were of two or more Hispanic subgroups, and 0.3 percent were of some other Hispanic subgroup.

More than two fifths of Hispanic adults (43.3 percent) were born in the United States.[4] U.S.-born Hispanic adults tended to be younger than those born in other countries; for example, 27.5 percent of Hispanic adults born in the United States and 14.5 percent of those born abroad were aged 18 to 25.

One third of Hispanic adults (33.9 percent) were without health insurance, a percentage higher than the national average of 15.0 percent for adults.[5]

Combined 2005 through 2008 data indicate that the poverty rate among Hispanics was twice as high as the national average for adults (22.3 vs. 11.5 percent).[6]

## Trends in Substance Use

The rate of past month alcohol use increased among Hispanic adults between 2004 and 2008 (43.7 vs. 47.6 percent) (Figure 1). Rates of binge alcohol use and illicit drug use did not change significantly among Hispanic adults over the 5-year period.[7,8]

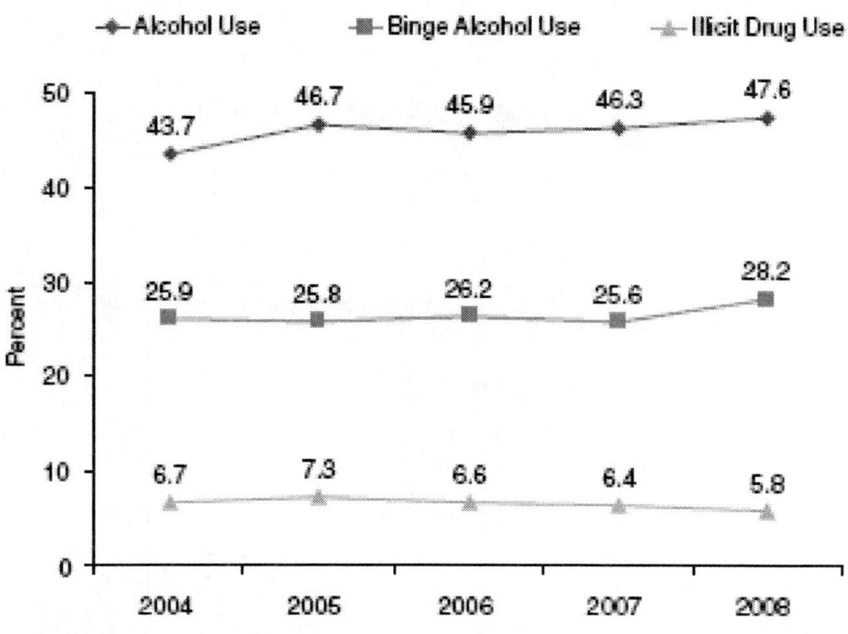


Source: 2004 to 2008 SAMHSA National Surveys on Drug Use and Health (NSDUHs).

Figure 1. Trends in Past Month Substance Use among Hispanic Adults: 2004 to 2008.

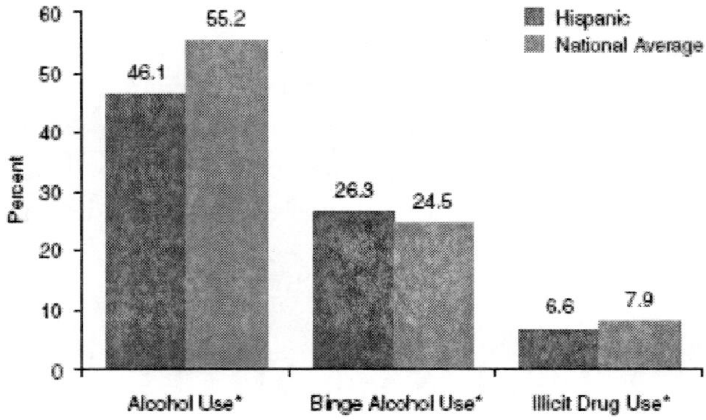


Source: 2004 to 2008 SAMHSA National Surveys on Drug Use and Health (NSDUHs).

* The difference between Hispanics and the national average is statistically significant at the .05 level.

Figure 2. Past Month Substance Use among Hispanic Adults Compared with the National Average for Adults: 2004 to 2008.

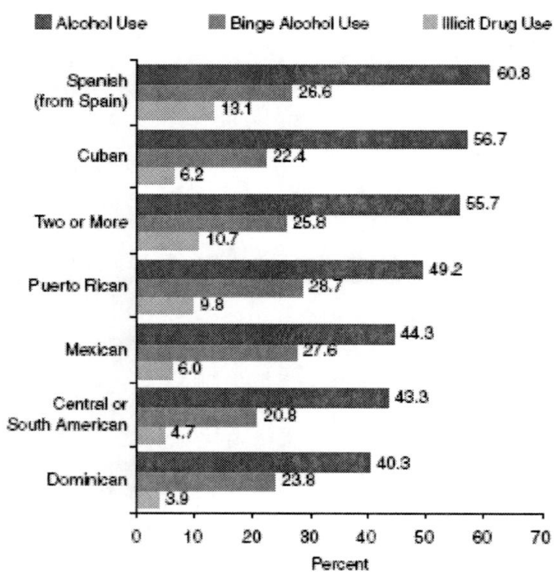


Source: 2004 to 2008 SAMHSA National Surveys on Drug Use and Health (NSDUHs).

* Estimates for the "Other, Hispanic" subgroup were suppressed due to low precision.

Figure 3. Past Month Substance Use among Hispanic Adults, by Hispanic Subgroup*: 2004 to 2008.

## PAST MONTH ALCOHOL AND ILLICIT DRUG USE

Combined 2004 to 2008 data indicate that, in the past month, 46.1 percent of Hispanic adults used alcohol, 26.3 percent engaged in binge alcohol use, and 6.6 percent used an illicit drug (Figure 2). Rates of past month alcohol use and illicit drug use were lower among Hispanic adults than the national averages. The rate of past month binge alcohol use among Hispanic adults, however, was higher than the national average.

## SUBSTANCE USE BY HISPANIC SUBGROUP

Among Hispanic adults, substance use varied greatly by subgroup. Past month alcohol use ranged from a high of 60.8 percent among adults of Spanish origin (from Spain) to a low of 40.3 percent among those of Dominican origin (Figure 3). Past month binge alcohol use ranged from a high of 28.7 percent among adults of Puerto Rican origin to a low of 20.8 percent among those of Central or South American origin, and illicit drug use ranged from a high of 13.1 percent among adults of Spanish origin to a low of 3.9 percent among those of Dominican origin.

## SUBSTANCE USE BY NATIVITY

Among Hispanic adults, those who were born in the United States had higher rates of past month alcohol use, binge alcohol use, and illicit drug use than those who were not born in the United States (Figure 4). These findings generally held within each age group that was examined (data not shown).

## SUBSTANCE USE AMONG YOUNG ADULTS (AGED 18 TO 25)

Rates of past month alcohol use, binge alcohol use, and illicit drug use were lower among young Hispanic adults than among young adults in the general population (50.5 vs. 61.1 percent, 35.8 vs. 41.6 percent, and 14.6 vs. 19.7 percent, respectively) (Figure 5).

## SUBSTANCE USE AMONG WOMEN

Compared with the national averages for women, adult Hispanic females had lower rates of past month alcohol use, binge alcohol use, and illicit drug use (Table 1). Patterns varied by age group.

Among women aged 18 to 44 who were pregnant at the time of the survey interview, Hispanics had lower rates of alcohol use and illicit drug use than the national average (5.9 vs. 11.2 percent and 2.5 vs. 4.0 percent, respectively) (Figure 6). The rate of past month binge alcohol use among pregnant Hispanic women did not differ significantly from the national average for pregnant women.

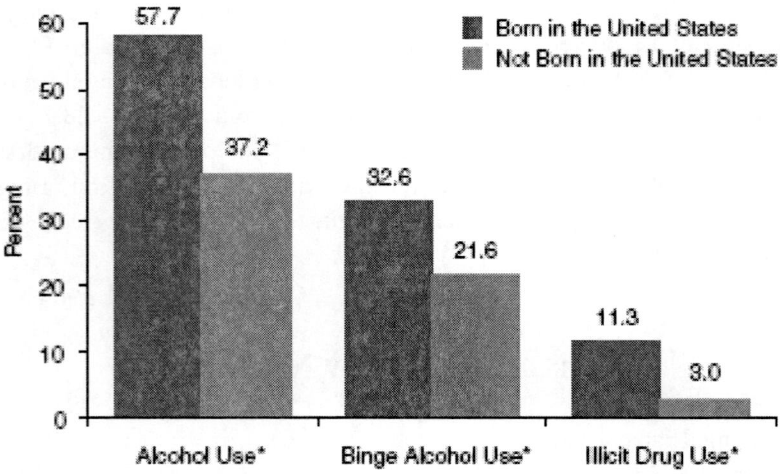


Source: 2004 to 2008 SAMHSA National Surveys on Drug Use and Health (NSDUHs).

* The difference between those born in the United States and those not born in the United States is statistically significant at the .05 level.

Figure 4. Past Month Substance Use among Hispanic Adults, by Nativity: 2004 to 2008.

## SUBSTANCE USE AMONG MEN

Compared with the national averages, adult Hispanic males had lower rates of past month alcohol use and illicit drug use but a higher rate of binge alcohol use (Table 2). Patterns varied by age group.

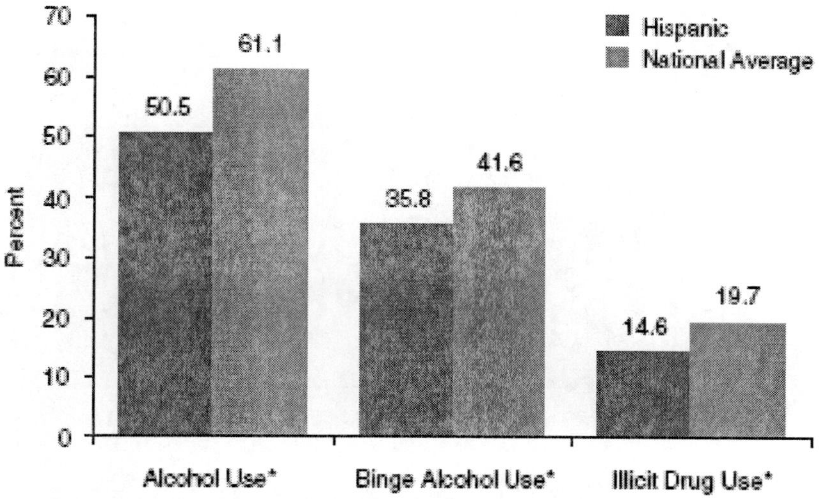


The difference between Hispanics and the national average is statistically significant at the .05 level.

Source: 2004 to 2008 SAMHSA National Surveys on Drug Use and Health (NSDUHs).

Figure 5. Past Month Substance Use among Hispanic Adults Aged 18 to 25 Compared with the National Average for Adults Aged 18 to 25: 2004 to 2008.

**Table 1. Past Month Substance Use among Hispanic Adult Females Compared with the National Average for Adult Females, by Age Group: Percentages, 2004 to 2008**

| Age Group | Alcohol Use | | Binge Alcohol Use | | Illicit Drug Use | |
|---|---|---|---|---|---|---|
| | Hispanics | National Average | Hispanics | National Average | Hispanics | National Average |
| Total | 36.1* | 48.5 | 15.0* | 15.9 | 4.5* | 5.7 |
| Aged 18 to 25 | 43.8* | 56.9 | 25.3* | 33.1 | 11.1* | 15.7 |
| Aged 26 to 49 | 38.0* | 53.7 | 15.5* | 18.9 | 3.7* | 6.2 |
| Aged 50 or Older | 26.5* | 40.1 | 6.2 | 6.6 | 1.1* | 1.8 |

* The difference between Hispanics and the national average is statistically significant at the .05 level.

Source: 2004 to 2008 SAMHSA National Surveys on Drug Use and Health (NSDUHs).

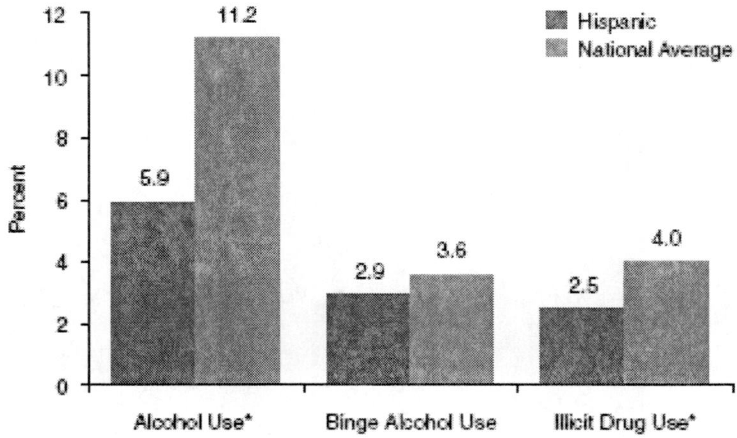


Source: 2004 to 2008 SAMHSA National Surveys on Drug Use and Health (NSDUHs).

The difference between Hispanics and the national average is statistically significant at the .05 level.

Figure 6. Past Month Substance Use among Hispanic Pregnant Women Aged 18 to 44 Compared with the National Average for Pregnant Women Aged 18 to 44: 2004 to 2008.

## SUBSTANCE USE AMONG UNINSURED PERSONS

Compared with the national averages for uninsured adults, uninsured Hispanic adults were less likely to have used alcohol, binged on alcohol, or used an illicit drug in the past month (41.5 vs. 52.3 percent, 28.3 vs. 33.1 percent, and 7.3 vs. 15.1 percent, respectively) (Figure 7).

## SUBSTANCE USE AMONG PERSONS LIVING IN POVERTY

The rates of past month alcohol use, binge alcohol use, and illicit drug use among Hispanic adults living in poverty were lower than the national averages for adults living in poverty (Figure 8).

**Table 2. Past Month Substance Use among Hispanic Adult Males Compared with the National Average for Adult Males, by Age Group: Percentages, 2004 to 2008**

| Age Group | Alcohol Use | | Binge Alcohol Use | | Illicit Drug Use | |
|---|---|---|---|---|---|---|
| | Hispanics | National Average | Hispanics | National Average | Hispanics | National Average |
| Total | 55.5* | 62.3 | 37.1* | 33.8 | 8.5* | 10.2 |
| Aged 18 to 25 | 56.4* | 65.3 | 45.2* | 50.0 | 17.7* | 23.8 |
| Aged 26 to 49 | 59.3* | 67.4 | 39.4 | 39.2 | 7.5* | 11.2 |
| Aged 50 or Older | 44.9* | 54.8 | 23.4 | 20.5 | 2.5 | 3.4 |

Source: 2004 to 2008 SAMHSA National Surveys on Drug Use and Health (NSDUHs).

* The difference between Hispanics and the national average is statistically significant at the .05 level.

## Alcohol Use Treatment

Combined 2004 to 2008 data indicate that an estimated 2.5 million Hispanic adults—8.7 percent—were classified as being in need of treatment for an alcohol use problem in the past year.[9] While the difference between the rate for Hispanics and the national average (8.7 versus 8.1 percent) was relatively small, it was statistically significant.

About 7.9 percent of Hispanic adults in need of alcohol treatment in the past year (195,000 persons) received it at a specialty facility.[10] This rate was similar to the national average (8.2 percent).

## Illicit Drug Use Treatment

An estimated 843,000 Hispanic adults—or 2.9 percent—were classified as being in need of treatment for an illicit drug use problem in the past year. This rate was similar to the national average of 2.9 percent.

About 18.3 percent of Hispanic adults in need of illicit drug treatment in the past year (155,000 persons) received it at a specialty facility. This rate was also similar to the national average.

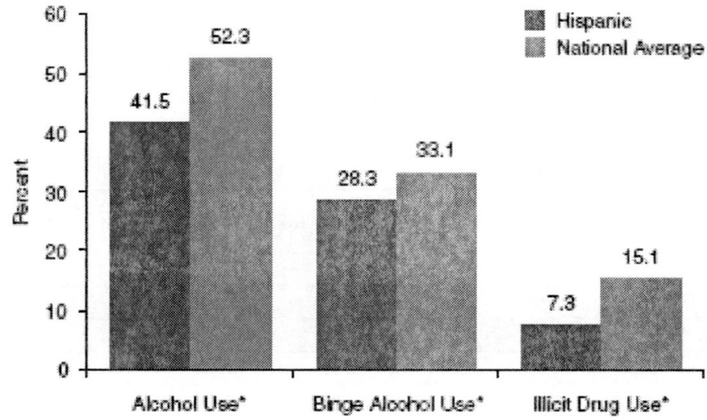


Source: 2004 to 2008 SAMHSA National Surveys on Drug Use and Health (NSDUHs).

* The difference between Hispanics and the national average is statistically significant at the .05 level.

Figure 7. Past Month Substance Use among Uninsured Hispanic Adults Compared with the National Average for Uninsured Adults: 2004 to 2008.

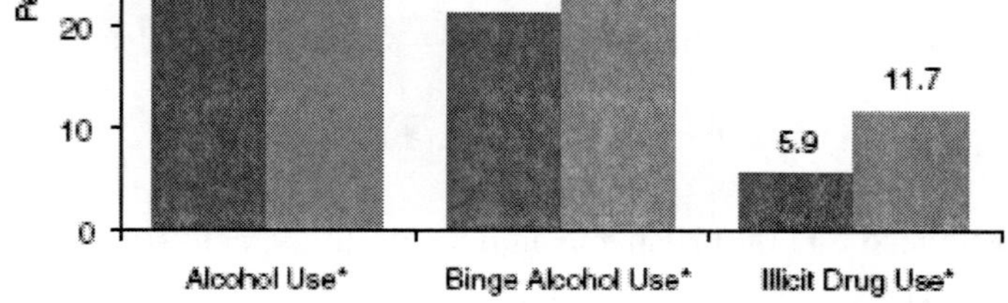


* The difference between Hispanics and the national average is statistically significant at the .05 level. Source: 2005 to 2008 SAMHSA National Surveys on Drug Use and Health (NSDUHs).

Figure 8. Past Month Substance Use among Hispanic Adults Living in Poverty Compared with the National Average for Adults Living in Poverty: 2005 to 2008.

## DISCUSSION

As the Federal Government and States move forward with the interrelated tasks of reducing disparities and reforming health care, it will be important to monitor data on substance use and treatment need among racial/ethnic minorities. The findings in this report highlight variations in substance use and treatment need between Hispanic adults and adults in the Nation as a whole and suggest subgroups that may benefit from increased attention from the prevention and treatment systems.

## NOTE

The National Survey on Drug Use and Health (NSDUH) is an annual survey sponsored by the Substance Abuse and Mental Health Services Administration (SAMHSA). The 2004 to 2008 data used in this report are based on information obtained from 227,791 persons aged 18 or older, including 31,848 Hispanics. The survey collects data by administering questionnaires to a representative sample of the population through face-to-face interviews at their place of residence.

## End Notes

[1] U.S. Census Bureau. (2008, August 14). An older and more diverse Nation by midcentury [U.S. Census Bureau News]. Retrieved January 11, 2010, from http://www.census.gov/Press-Release/www/releases/archives/ population/012496.html.

[2] NSDUH asks a series of questions about race/ethnicity. First, respondents are asked about their Hispanic origin; then they are asked to identify which racial grouping best describes them: white, black/African American, American Indian or Alaska Native, Native Hawaiian, other Pacific Islander, Asian, or other. Respondents may select more than one race. For this report, respondents identifying themselves as Hispanic were assigned to the Hispanic group regardless of their racial identification. Individuals who identify themselves as Hispanic are asked to name a Hispanic subgroup that best describes them; response options include Mexican/Mexican American/Mexicano/Chicano, Puerto Rican, Central or South American, Cuban/Cuban American, Dominican (from the Dominican Republic), Spanish (from Spain), and other. Respondents may select more than one Hispanic subgroup.

[3] Numbers were calculated from various census tables: U.S. Census Bureau. (2009, December 22). National characteristics. Retrieved January 11, 2010, from http://www.census.gov/ popest/national/asrh/natasrh.html.

[4] Respondents were asked if they were born in the United States, and responses to this question were used to differentiate U.S.-born versus foreign-born Hispanics. All findings in this

report pertain strictly to residents of the United States, not to persons living in other countries. No information is collected on citizenship; thus, no inferences can be made in this regard.

[5] A respondent is classified as having health insurance coverage if he or she has private insurance, Medicare, Medicaid/Children's Health Insurance Program (CHIP), Civilian Health and Medical Program of the Uniformed Services (CHAMPUS), TRICARE, Civilian Health and Medical Program of the Department of Veterans Affairs (CHAMPVA), Veterans Affairs (VA), military health care, or any other type of health insurance. All other respondents were classified as without health insurance or uninsured.

[6] NSDUH gathers data on family income, size, and composition (i.e., number of children) and respondent's age. This information is used to determine the respondent's poverty level. The poverty level is calculated as a percentage of the U.S. Census Bureau's poverty threshold by dividing the respondent's reported total family income by the appropriate poverty threshold amount. If a family's total income is less than the family's poverty threshold, then that family and every individual in it is considered to be living in poverty (i.e., less than 100 percent of the U.S. Census Bureau's poverty threshold). Persons aged 18 to 22 living in college dormitories were excluded from this analysis because poverty status is not determined for this group. The poverty variable is available for the years from 2005 to 2008; therefore, information for this estimate is restricted to combined data from these years.

[7] Binge alcohol use is defined as drinking five or more drinks on the same occasion (i.e., at the same time or within a couple of hours of each other) on at least 1 day in the past 30 days.

[8] NSDUH defines illicit drugs as marijuana/hashish, cocaine (including crack), inhalants, hallucinogens, heroin, or prescription-type drugs used nonmedically. Nonmedical use is defined as the use of prescription-type drugs not prescribed for the respondent by a physician or used only for the experience or feeling they caused. Nonmedical use of any prescription-type pain reliever, sedative, stimulant, or tranquilizer does not include over-the-counter drugs; nonmedical use of stimulants includes methamphetamine use.

[9] NSDUH classifies persons as needing treatment for alcohol or illicit drug use if they meet the criteria for dependence or abuse or if they received specialty treatment in the past year. NSDUH defines substance dependence or abuse using criteria specified in the Diagnostic and Statistical Manual of Mental Disorders (DSM-IV), including symptoms such as withdrawal, tolerance, use in dangerous situations, trouble with the law, and interference in major obligations at work, school, or home during the past year. For details, see the following resource: American Psychiatric Association. (1994). Diagnostic and statistical manual of mental disorders (4th ed.). Washington, DC: Author.

[10] Substance use treatment at a specialty facility is defined as treatment received at drug or alcohol rehabilitation facilities (inpatient or outpatient), hospitals (inpatient services only), and mental health centers; it excludes treatment received in an emergency room, private doctor's office, self-help group, prison or jail, or hospital as an outpatient.31.121.35. 939.825.211.701020304050.

In: Substance Use Among Select Ethnicities
Editor: Ron N. Gurovitz
ISBN: 978-1-62808-631-7


*Chapter 4*

# THE NSDUH REPORT: SUBSTANCE USE AMONG ASIAN ADULTS*

## *National Survey on Drug Use and Health*

## IN BRIEF

- Rates of past month alcohol use, binge alcohol use, and illicit drug use were lower among Asian adults than the national averages (39.8 vs. 55.2 percent, 13.2 vs. 24.5 percent, and 3.4 vs. 7.9 percent, respectively)
- Among Asian adults, substance use varied greatly among Asian subgroups; past month binge alcohol use, for example, ranged from a high of 25.9 percent among Korean adults to a low of 8.4 percent among Chinese adults
- Among Asian adults, those who were born in the United States generally had higher rates of past month substance use than those who were not born in the United States, regardless of age
- The percentage who needed treatment for a substance use problem in the past year was lower among Asian adults than for the national average of adults (4.8 vs. 9.6 percent)

* This report (NSDUH 179) was released by the Substance Abuse and Mental Health Services Administration, Office of Applied Studies, May 20, 2010.

Over the past several decades, the population of the United States has become increasingly diverse. According to the U.S. Census Bureau, about one third of the population belongs to a racial/ethnic minority group; this percentage is projected to increase to 54 percent by 2050.[1] As the country becomes more diverse, it becomes increasingly important to address health and health care disparities related to race/ethnicity, as well as age and gender, socioeconomic status, geography, and disability. The Nation's success in reducing these disparities today, to a large extent, will determine the health of our Nation tomorrow.

One area of concern is assessing substance use and abuse and ensuring access to substance abuse treatment. Substance abuse affects millions of people every year and imposes untold health, social, and economic costs on individuals, families, and communities. Although it affects people in all racial/ethnic groups, research has shown that there is considerable variation among these groups. Gaining a better understanding of the behavioral health needs of particular racial/ethnic groups can help inform public health policy, build prevention and treatment programs that target the different needs of these populations, and expand access to services for individuals who need them.

This report uses data from the National Survey on Drug Use and Health (NSDUH) to examine substance use and treatment need among non-Hispanic Asian (hereafter referred to as Asian) adults aged 18 or older.[2] Other reports in this series will examine similar issues among Asian adolescents and among adults and adolescents in other racial/ethnic groups. According to the U.S. Census Bureau, 13 million people—4.4 percent of the total U.S. resident population in 2008—identify themselves as non-Hispanic Asians of one race.[3] This report is based on NSDUH data from 2004 to 2008.

## Demographic Characteristics

Combined 2004 to 2008 data indicate that almost one in four (24.0 percent) Asians reported being Asian Indian, 23.1 percent were Chinese, 21.1 percent were Filipino, 8.9 percent were Japanese, 7.7 percent were Vietnamese, and 7.6 percent were Korean.

About one fifth of Asian adults (19.1 percent) were born in the United States.[4] U.S.-born Asian adults tended to be younger than those born in other countries; for example, 35.1 percent of Asian adults born in the United States were aged 18 to 25 compared with 11.6 percent of Asian adults born abroad.

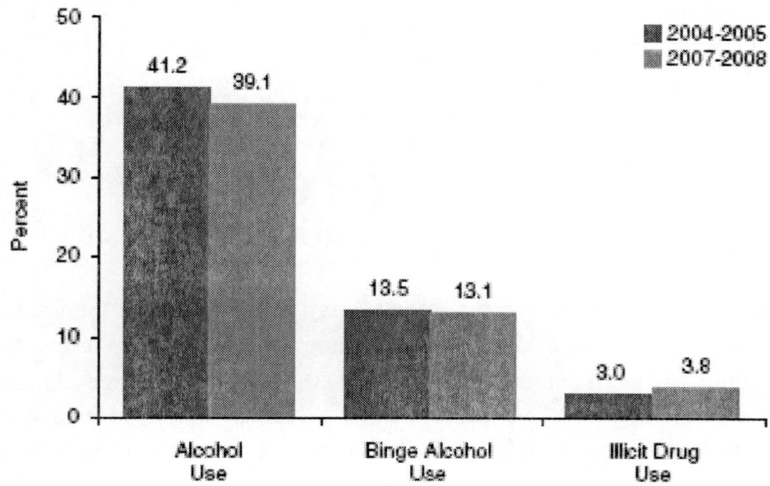


Source: 2004, 2005, 2007, and 2008 SAMHSA National Surveys on Drug Use and Health (NSDUHs).

Figure 1. Past Month Substance Use among Asians Aged 18 or Older: 2004-2005 versus 2007-2008.

Nearly one seventh of Asian adults (13.3 percent) were without health insurance, a percentage lower than the national average of 15.0 percent for adults.[5]

Combined 2005 through 2008 data indicate that the poverty rate among Asians did not differ significantly from the national average (11.5 and 10.9 percent, respectively).[6]

## Trends in Substance Use

Among Asian adults, rates of past month alcohol use, binge alcohol use, and illicit drug use in combined 2007 and 2008 were not significantly different from rates in combined 2004 and 2005 (Figure 1).[7,8]

## Past Month Alcohol and Illicit Drug Use

Combined 2004 to 2008 data indicate that, in the past month, 39.8 percent of Asian adults used alcohol, 13.2 percent engaged in binge alcohol use, and

3.4 percent used an illicit drug (Figure 2). Rates of past month alcohol use, binge alcohol use, and illicit drug use were lower among Asian adults than the national averages for adults.

## SUBSTANCE USE AMONG ASIAN SUBGROUPS

Substance use varied greatly among Asian subgroups. Past month alcohol use ranged from a high of 51.9 percent among Korean adults to a low of 32.1 percent among Asian Indian adults (Figure 3). Past month binge alcohol use ranged from a high of 25.9 percent among Korean adults to a low of 8.4 percent among Chinese adults, and illicit drug use ranged from a high of 6.2 percent among Japanese adults to a low of 2.1 percent among Chinese and Asian Indian adults.

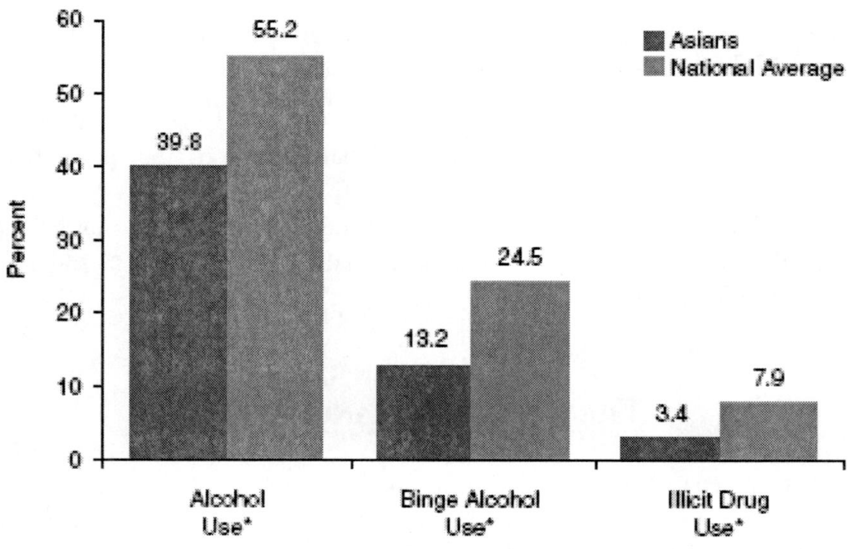


Source: 2004 to 2008 SAMHSA National Surveys on Drug Use and Health (NSDUHs).

* The difference between Asians and the national average is statistically significant at the .05 level.

Figure 2. Past Month Substance Use among Asians Aged 18 or Older Compared with the National Average: 2004 to 2008.

## SUBSTANCE USE BY NATIVITY

Among Asian adults, those who were born in the United States had higher rates of past month alcohol use, binge alcohol use, and illicit drug use than those who were not born in the United States (Table 1). These patterns held within each age group for which estimates could be generated, although not all differences were statistically significant.

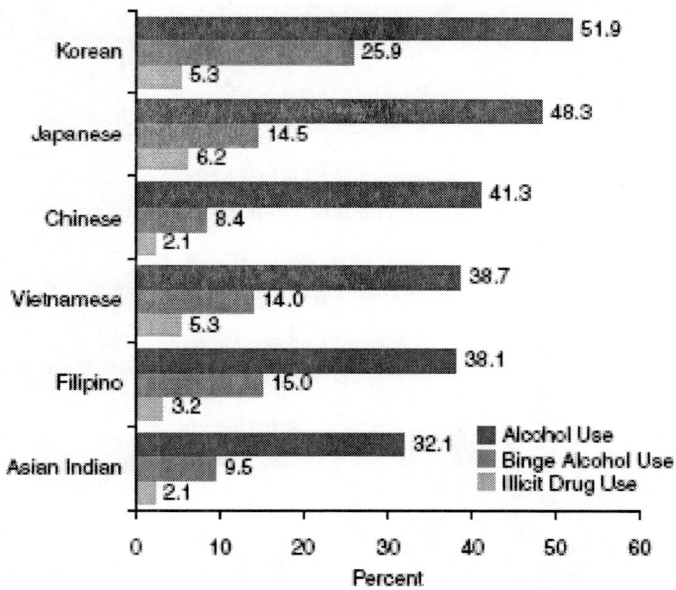


Source: 2004 to 2008 SAMHSA National Surveys on Drug Use and Health (NSDUHs).

Figure 3. Past Month Substance Use among Asians Aged 18 or Older, by Asian Subgroup: 2004 to 2008.

## SUBSTANCE USE AMONG YOUNG ADULTS (AGED 18 TO 25)

Rates of past month alcohol use, binge alcohol use, and illicit drug use were considerably lower among young Asian adults than the national average for young adults (48.5 vs. 61.1 percent, 25.7 vs. 41.6 percent, and 9.1 vs. 19.7 percent, respectively) (Figure 4).

**Table 1. Past Month Substance Use among Asians Aged 18 or Older, by Nativity: Percentages, 2004 to 2008**

| | Alcohol Use | | Binge Alcohol Use | | Illicit Drug Use | |
|---|---|---|---|---|---|---|
| Age Group | Born in the United States | Not Born in the United States | Born in the United States | Not Born in the United States | Born in the United States | Not Born in the United States |
| Total | 56.0* | 35.9 | 22.0* | 11.1 | 7.3* | 2.5 |
| Aged 18 to 25 | 54.0* | 44.6 | 31.4* | 21.6 | 12.2* | 7.0 |
| Aged 26 to 49 | 68.0* | 38.3 | 23.3* | 10.9 | 5.0* | 1.8 |
| Aged 50 or Older | 42.1* | 28.0 | 8.3 | 7.4 | ** | 2.0 |

Source: 2004 to 2008 SAMHSA National Surveys on Drug Use and Health (NSDUHs).

* The difference between Asians born in the United States and not born in the United States is statistically significant at the .05 level. ** Estimate was suppressed because of low precision.

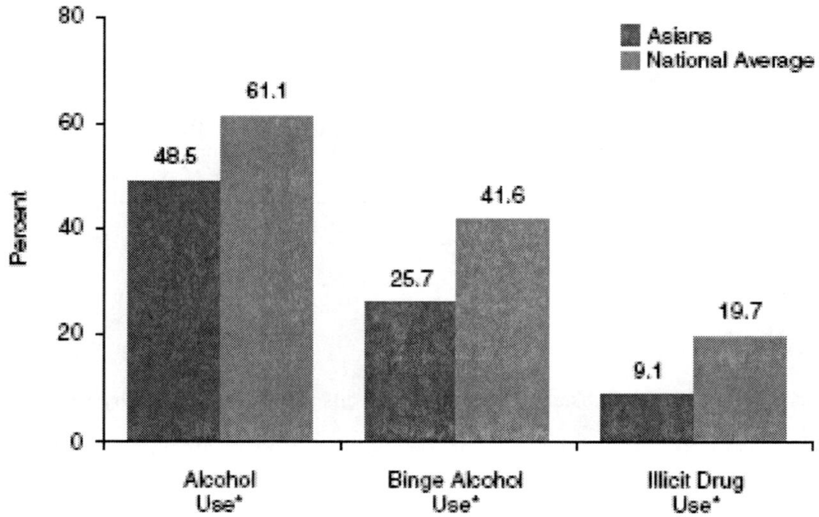


* The difference between Asians and the national average is statistically significant at the .05 level.

Source: 2004 to 2008 SAMHSA National Surveys on Drug Use and Health (NSDUHs).

Figure 4. Past Month Substance Use among Young Asian Adults Aged 18 to 25 Compared with the National Average: 2004 to 2008.

## SUBSTANCE USE AMONG WOMEN

Compared with the national averages for adult females, adult Asian females had lower rates of past month alcohol use, binge alcohol use, and illicit drug use (Table 2).

This pattern held within most age groups.

**Table 2. Past Month Substance Use among Asian Females Aged 18 or Older Compared with the National Average, by Age Group: Percentages, 2004 to 2008**

| Age Group | Alcohol Use | | Binge Alcohol Use | | Illicit Drug Use | |
|---|---|---|---|---|---|---|
| | Asians | National Average | Asians | National Average | Asians | National Average |
| Total | 29.6* | 48.5 | 7.7* | 15.9 | 2.9* | 5.7 |
| Aged 18 to 25 | 43.6* | 56.9 | 19.6* | 33.1 | 6.9* | 15.7 |
| Aged 26 to 49 | 32.0* | 53.7 | 7.0* | 18.9 | 1.4* | 6.2 |
| Aged 50 or Older | 18.3* | 40.1 | 3.1* | 6.6 | 3.5 | 1.8 |

Source: 2004 to 2008 SAMHSA National Surveys on Drug Use and Health (NSDUHs).

* The difference between Asians and the national average is statistically significant at the .05 level.

**Table 3. Past Month Substance Use among Asian Males Aged 18 or Older Compared with the National Average, by Age Group: Percentages, 2004 to 2008**

| Age Group | Alcohol Use | | Binge Alcohol Use | | Illicit Drug Use | |
|---|---|---|---|---|---|---|
| | Asians | National Average | Asians | National Average | Asians | National Average |
| Total | 51.1* | 62.3 | 19.2* | 33.8 | 3.9* | 10.2 |
| Aged 18 to 25 | 53.5* | 65.3 | 31.8* | 50.0 | 11.4* | 23.8 |
| Aged 26 to 49 | 53.6* | 67.4 | 18.6* | 39.2 | 3.1* | 11.2 |
| Aged 50 or Older | 45.0* | 54.8 | 12.8* | 20.5 | 1.0* | 3.4 |

Source: 2004 to 2008 SAMHSA National Surveys on Drug Use and Health (NSDUHs).* The difference between Asians and the national average is statistically significant at the .05 level.

## Substance Use among Men

Compared with the national averages for adult males, adult Asian males had lower rates of past month alcohol use, binge alcohol use, and illicit drug use (Table 3). This pattern held within most age groups, and most comparisons were statistically significant.

## Substance Use among Uninsured Persons

Uninsured Asian adults were less likely than the national average for uninsured adults to have used alcohol in the past month (35.2 vs. 52.3 percent), to have binged on alcohol in the past month (18.6 vs. 33.1 percent), and to have used illicit drugs in the past month (6.6 vs. 15.1 percent) (Figure 5).

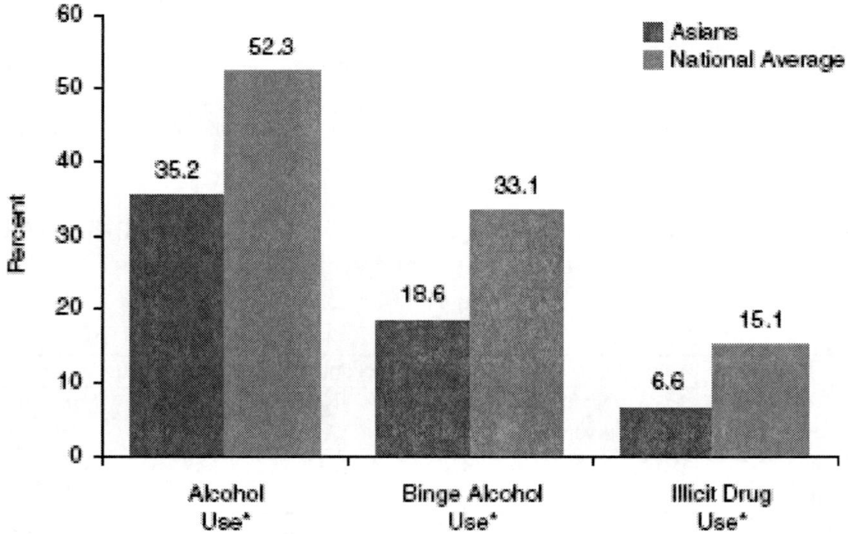


Source: 2004 to 2008 SAMHSA National Surveys on Drug Use and Health (NSDUHs).

* The difference between Asians and the national average is statistically significant at the .05 level.

Figure 5. Past Month Substance Use among Asians Aged 18 or Older Who Were Uninsured Compared with the National Average: 2004 to 2008.

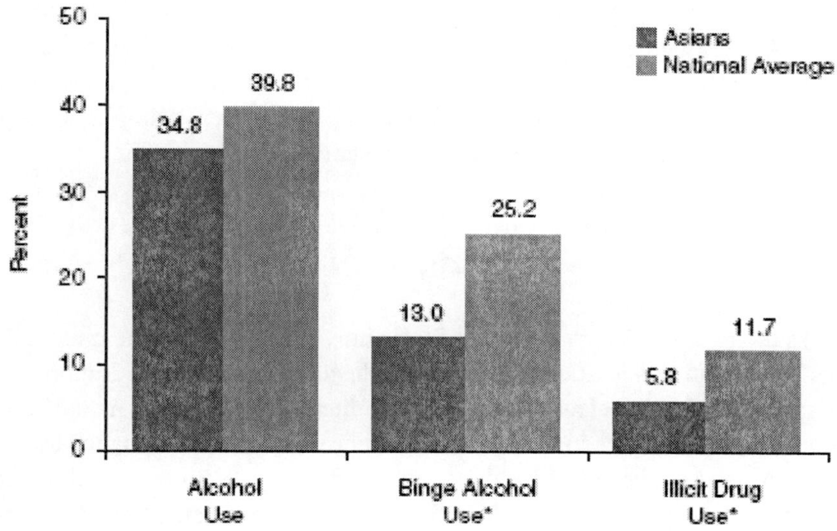


Source: 2005 to 2008 SAMHSA National Surveys on Drug Use and Health (NSDUHs).

* The difference between Asians and the national average is statistically significant at the .05 level.

Figure 6. Past Month Substance Use among Asians Aged 18 or Older Living in Poverty Compared with the National Average: 2005 to 2008.

## SUBSTANCE USE AMONG PERSONS LIVING IN POVERTY

The rates of past month binge alcohol use and illicit drug use among Asian adults living in poverty were lower than the national average for adults living in poverty (13.0 vs. 25.2 percent and 5.8 vs. 11.7 percent, respectively); the rate of past month alcohol use among Asian adults living in poverty, however, did not differ significantly from the national average (Figure 6).

## TREATMENT NEED

Combined 2004 to 2008 data indicate that an estimated 451,000 Asian adults—4.8 percent— were classified as being in need of treatment for a substance use problem in the past year.[9] This rate was lower than the national average of 9.6 percent for adults. Of Asian adults in need of substance use treatment in the past year (28,000 persons), 1 in 16 (6.1 percent) received it at a specialty facility.[10] Although this rate appears lower than the national average (10.4 percent), the difference is not statistically significant.

## Discussion

As the Federal Government and States move forward with the interrelated tasks of reducing disparities and reforming health care, it will be important to monitor data on substance use and treatment need among racial/ethnic minorities. The findings in this report highlight variations in substance use and treatment need between Asian adults and adults in the Nation as a whole and suggest subgroups that may benefit from increased attention from the prevention and treatment systems.

## Note

The National Survey on Drug Use and Health (NSDUH) is an annual survey sponsored by the Substance Abuse and Mental Health Services Administration (SAMHSA). The 2004 to 2008 data used in this report are based on information obtained from 227,791 persons aged 18 or older, including 7,629 Asian adults. The survey collects data by administering questionnaires to a representative sample of the population through face-to-face interviews at their place of residence.

## End Notes

[1] U.S. Census Bureau. (2008, August 14). An older and more diverse Nation by midcentury [U.S. Census Bureau News]. Retrieved January 11, 2010, from http://www.census.gov/ Press-Release/www/releases/archives/ population/012496.html.

[2] NSDUH asks a series of questions about race/ethnicity. First, respondents are asked about their Hispanic origin; then they are asked to identify which racial grouping(s) best describes them: white, black or African American, American Indian, Alaska Native, Native Hawaiian, Other Pacific Islander, Asian, or other. Individuals who identify themselves as Asian also are asked to name an Asian subgrouping that best describes them; response options include Asian Indian, Chinese, Filipino, Japanese, Korean, Vietnamese, and other. Respondents

may select more than one race. For this report, "Asian" refers to persons identifying themselves as Asian only. Persons identifying as Asian and Hispanic or Asian and another racial group are not included.

[3] Numbers were calculated from various census tables: U.S. Census Bureau. (2009, December 22). National characteristics. Retrieved January 11, 2010, from http://www.census.gov/popest/national/asrh/natasrh.html

[4] Respondents were asked if they were born in the United States, and responses to this question were used to differentiate U.S.-born Asians from foreign-born Asians. All findings in this report pertain strictly to residents of the United States, not to persons living in other countries. No information is collected on citizenship.

[5] A respondent is classified as having health insurance coverage if he or she has private insurance, Medicare, Medicaid/Children's Health Insurance Program (CHIP), Civilian Health and Medical Program of the Uniformed Services (CHAMPUS), TRICARE, Civilian Health and Medical Program of the Department of Veterans Affairs (CHAMPVA), Veterans Affairs (VA), military health care, or any other type of health insurance. All other respondents were classified as without health insurance or uninsured.

[6] NSDUH gathers data on family income, size, and composition (i.e., number of children) and respondent's age. This information is used to determine the respondent's poverty level. The poverty level is calculated as a percentage of the U.S. Census Bureau's poverty threshold by dividing the respondent's reported total family income by the appropriate poverty threshold amount. If a family's total income is less than the family's poverty threshold, then that family and every individual in it is considered to be living in poverty (i.e., less than 100 percent of the U.S. census poverty threshold). Persons aged 18 to 22 living in college dormitories were excluded from this analysis because poverty status is not determined for this group. The poverty variable is available for the years from 2005 to 2008; therefore, information for this estimate is restricted to combined data from these years.

[7] Binge alcohol use is defined as drinking five or more drinks on the same occasion (i.e., at the same time or within a couple of hours of each other) on at least 1 day in the past 30 days.

[8] NSDUH defines illicit drugs as marijuana/hashish, cocaine (including crack), inhalants, hallucinogens, heroin, or prescription-type drugs used nonmedically. Nonmedical use is defined as the use of prescription-type drugs not prescribed for the respondent by a physician or used only for the experience or feeling they caused. Nonmedical use of any prescription-type pain reliever, sedative, stimulant, or tranquilizer does not include over-the-counter drugs; nonmedical use of stimulants includes methamphetamine use.

[9] NSDUH classifies persons as needing treatment for alcohol or illicit drug use if they meet the criteria for dependence or abuse or if they received specialty treatment in the past year. NSDUH defines substance dependence or abuse using criteria specified in the Diagnostic and Statistical Manual of Mental Disorders (DSM-IV), including symptoms such as withdrawal, tolerance, use in dangerous situations, trouble with the law, and interference in major obligations at work, school, or home during the past year. For details, see the following resource: American Psychiatric Association. (1994). Diagnostic and statistical manual of mental disorders (4th ed.). Washington, DC: Author.

[10] Substance use treatment at a specialty facility is defined as treatment received at drug or alcohol rehabilitation facilities (inpatient or outpatient), hospitals (inpatient services only), and mental health centers; it excludes treatment received in an emergency room, private doctor's office, self-help group, prison or jail, or hospital as an outpatient.

In: Substance Use Among Select Ethnicities ISBN: 978-1-62808-631-7
Editor: Ron N. Gurovitz 

*Chapter 5*

# THE NSDUH REPORT: SUBSTANCE USE AMONG BLACK ADOLESCENTS*

## *National Survey on Drug Use and Health*

## IN BRIEF

- Compared with the national average for adolescents aged 12 to 17, black adolescents had lower rates of past month cigarette use (5.8 vs. 10.2 percent), alcohol use (10.5 vs. 16.0 percent), marijuana use (6.5 vs. 6.9 percent), and nonmedical use of prescription-type drugs (2.9 vs. 3.3 percent)
- The rate of marijuana use among black adolescents increased from 5.9 percent in 2008 to 7.5 percent in 2010
- The rates of past month cigarette use and alcohol use among black adolescents living in poverty were lower than the national averages for adolescents living in poverty (6.8 vs. 10.6 percent and 10.7 vs. 13.5 percent, respectively)

Black or African American adolescents have generally been shown to have lower rates of substance use than white adolescents. Researchers have suggested that family attitudes and behaviors that discourage drug use may

---

* This report (NSDUH 004) was released by the Substance Abuse and Mental Health Services Administration, Office of Applied Studies, October 4, 2011.

contribute to the relatively low rates of drug use observed among black youths.[1]

However, despite the lower drug use rates in adolescence, rates of drug use among black adults closely mirror or exceed those among white adults.[2] Since initiation of drug use typically occurs before the age of 25,[3] efforts to prevent, delay, or reduce drug use among black youths, particularly efforts that target the critical period of late adolescence, may have longterm implications for improvements in behavioral and physical health, education, and employment outcomes among this population.

This report examines substance use among non-Hispanic black or African American adolescents (hereafter referred to as "black adolescents") aged 12 to 17.[4]

Combined data from the 2004 to 2009 National Surveys of Drug Use and Health (NSDUHs) are used when discussing estimates, while trends are discussed using data from the 2002 to 2010 NSDUHs. The report presented here is one in a series of reports intended to describe adolescent substance use within racial and ethnic subpopulations of the United States.

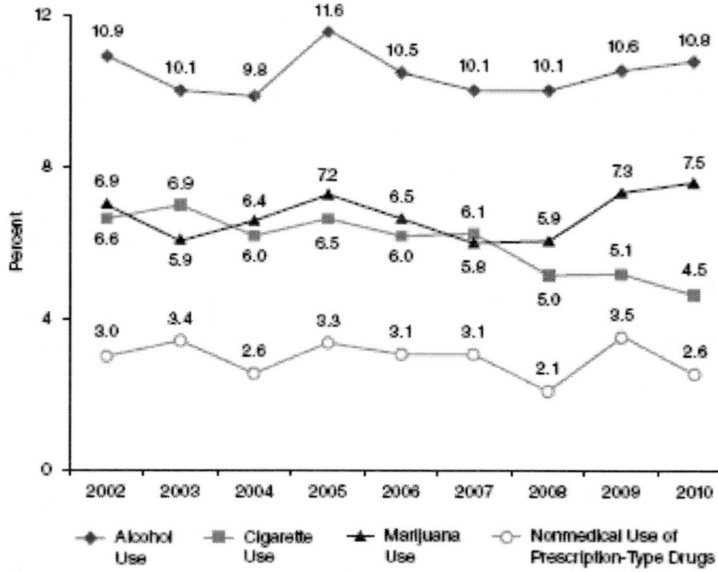


Source: 2002 to 2010 SAMHSA National Surveys on Drug Use and Health (NSDUHs).

Figure 1. Trends in Past Month Substance Use among Blacks Aged 12 to 17: 2002 to 2010.

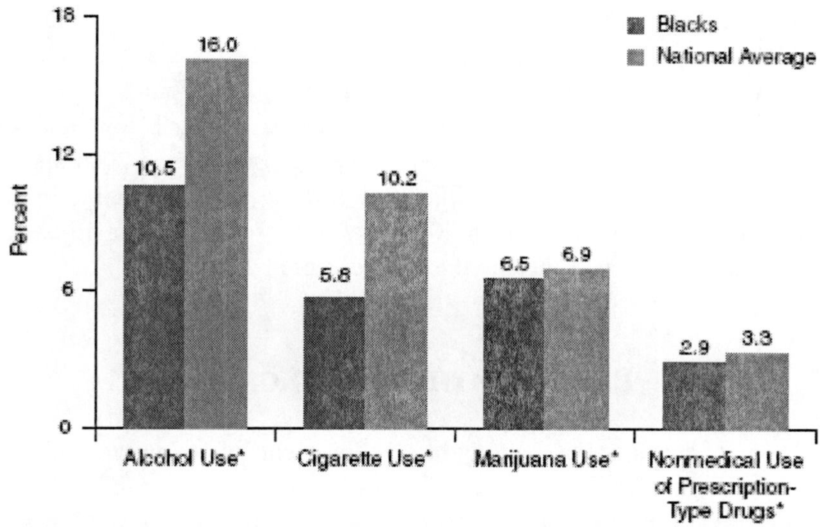


* The difference between blacks and the national average is statistically significant at the .05 level. Source: 2004 to 2009 SAMHSA National Surveys on Drug Use and Health (NSDUHs).

Figure 2. Past Month Substance Use among Blacks Aged 12 to 17 Compared with the National Average: 2004 to 2009.

## Demographic Characteristics

Combined 2004 to 2009 NSDUH data indicate that an annual average of 3.8 million persons aged 12 to 17—15.2 percent of the total population in this age group—identified themselves as non-Hispanic blacks of one race. Black adolescents were similar to the national average in terms of age and gender distributions. Compared with the national average, however, black adolescents were nearly twice as likely to be living in poverty (35.4 vs. 18.1 percent) and were more likely to live in large metropolitan areas (65.1 vs. 53.5 percent).[5]

## Trends in Substance Use

The rate of past month cigarette use among black adolescents decreased from 6.6 percent in 2002 to 4.5 percent in 2010 (Figure 1).

Past month alcohol use was fairly stable from 2002 to 2010. Nonmedical use of prescription type drugs among black adolescents was also relatively stable from 2002 to 2007. However, after a drop to 2.1 percent in 2008, the rate of nonmedical use of prescription-type drugs among black adolescents rose to 3.5 percent in 2009; the difference between the rate in 2009 and 2010 was not statistically significant.6 Finally, following a steady decline from 7.2 percent in 2005 to 5.9 percent in 2008, the rate of past month marijuana use among black adolescents increased to 7.5 percent in 2010.

## PAST MONTH SUBSTANCE USE

Rates of substance use among black adolescents were lower than national averages (Figure 2). The greatest differences were for rates of past month alcohol use (10.5 vs. 16.0 percent) and cigarette use (5.8 vs. 10.2 percent). Smaller (but statistically significant) differences were found for marijuana use (6.5 vs. 6.9 percent) and nonmedical use of prescription-type drugs (2.9 vs. 3.3 percent).

## SUBSTANCE USE, BY AGE GROUP

Among younger black adolescents aged 12 to 14, the rates of past month alcohol use and cigarette use were lower than the national averages (Table 1). Similarly, rates of alcohol and cigarette use also were lower among black adolescents aged 15 to 17 than the national averages. The rate of past month nonmedical use of prescriptiontype drugs among adolescents aged 12 to 14 was higher for blacks than the national average (2.9 vs. 2.0 percent); however, among adolescents aged 15 to 17, rates were lower among black adolescents than the national average (3.0 vs. 4.4 percent).

Figure 3 shows the dynamic interaction taking place between age and race/ethnicity for marijuana use. Black adolescents aged 12 to 14 had a rate of past month marijuana use that was similar to the national average for that age group (1.8 vs. 2.0 percent). The rate was lower among black adolescents aged 15 to 17 than the national average for that age group, and the black and national average rates were similar for young adults aged 18 to 23. However, marijuana use rates among blacks exceeded the national average for adults aged 24 to 26, 27 to 29, and 30 to 39.

## SUBSTANCE USE, BY GENDER

Compared with the national averages for adolescent females, adolescent black females had lower rates of past month substance use (Figure 4).

Black male adolescents also were less likely than male adolescents in the Nation as a whole to have used alcohol (10.2 vs. 15.8 percent) and cigarettes (6.3 vs. 10.0 percent) in the past month, but differences in rates of marijuana use and nonmedical use of prescription-type drugs were not statistically significant.

**Table 1. Past Month Substance Use among Blacks Aged 12 to 17 Compared with the National Average, by Age Group: 2004 to 2009**

| | Alcohol Use | | Cigarette Use | | Nonmedical Use of Prescription-Type Drugs | |
|---|---|---|---|---|---|---|
| | Blacks | National Average | Blacks | National Average | Blacks | National Average |
| Age Group | (%) | (%) | (%) | (%) | (%) | (%) |
| Aged 12-14 | 4.5* | 6.2 | 1.9* | 3.5 | 2.9* | 2.0 |
| Aged 15-17 | 16.1* | 25.4 | 9.5* | 16.5 | 3.0* | 4.4 |

Source: 2004 to 2009 SAMHSA National Surveys on Drug Use and Health (NSDUHs).

* The difference between blacks and the national average is statistically significant at the .05 level.

## SUBSTANCE USE AMONG ADOLESCENTS LIVING IN POVERTY

The rates of past month cigarette use and alcohol use among black adolescents living in poverty were lower than the national averages for adolescents living in poverty (6.8 vs. 10.6 percent and 10.7 vs. 13.5 percent, respectively).

Rates of past month marijuana use and nonmedical use of prescription-type drugs, however, did not differ significantly from the national averages for adolescents living in poverty (Figure 5).

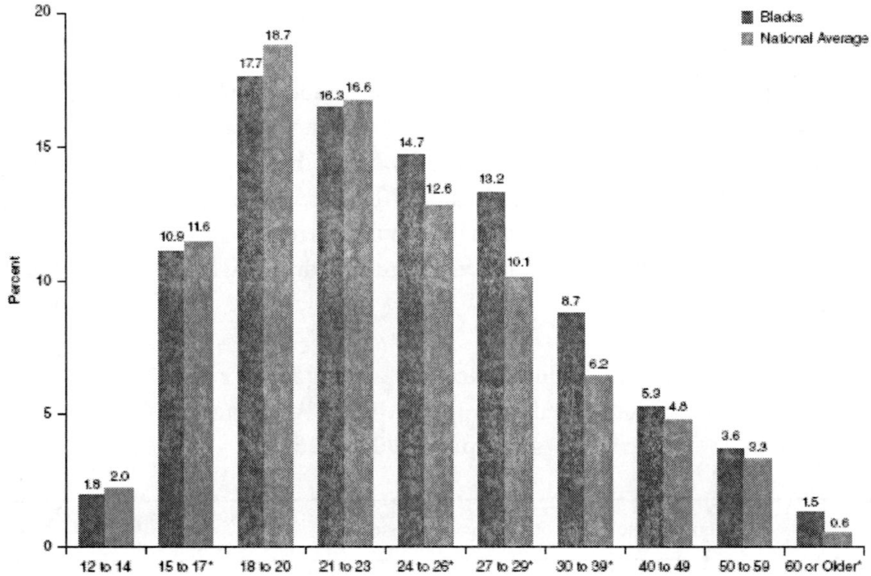


Source: 2004 to 2009 SAMHSA National Surveys on Drug Use and Health (NSDUHs).

* The difference between blacks and the national average is statistically significant at the .05 level.

Figure 3. Past Month Marijuana Use among Blacks Compared with the National Average, by Age Group: 2004 to 2009.

## Discussion

This report confirms that substance use rates are generally lower among black adolescents than national rates for adolescents; however, the recent increases in marijuana use and in the nonmedical use of prescription-type drugs among black adolescents highlight the need for treatment programs and prevention strategies that target black adolescents.

Those designing and implementing prevention programs should also be aware of the higher rates of marijuana use among blacks aged 24 or older compared with the national averages, suggesting the need for efforts specifically tailored to the prevention of marijuana initiation for black adolescents.

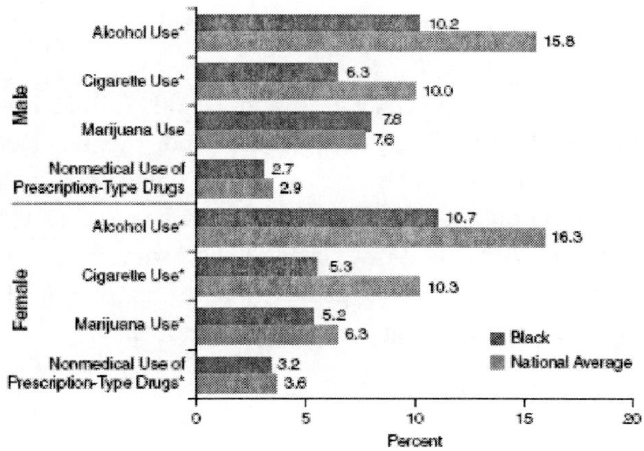


Source: 2004 to 2009 SAMHSA National Surveys on Drug Use and Health (NSDUHs).

* The difference between blacks and the national average is statistically significant at the .05 level.

Figure 4. Past Month Substance Use among Black Adolescents Aged 12 to 17 Compared with the National Average, by Gender: 2004 to 2009.

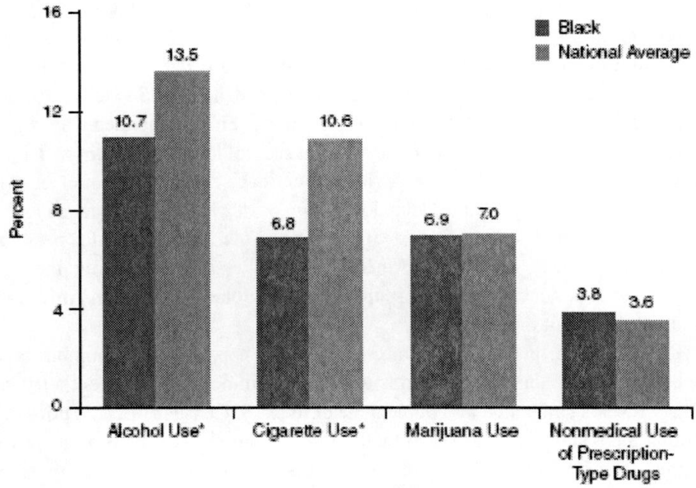


Source: 2005 to 2009 SAMHSA National Surveys on Drug Use and Health (NSDUHs).

* The difference between blacks and the national average is statistically significant at the .05 level.

Figure 5. Past Month Substance Use among Blacks Aged 12 to 17 Living in Poverty Compared with the National Average Living in Poverty: 2005 to 2009.

# NOTE

The National Survey on Drug Use and Health (NSDUH) is an annual survey sponsored by the Substance Abuse and Mental Health Services Administration (SAMHSA). The 2004 to 2009 data used in this report are based on information obtained from 135,311 persons aged 12 to 17, including 18,341 blacks or African Americans. The survey collects data by administering questionnaires to a representative sample of the population through face-to-face interviews at their place of residence.

## End Notes

[1] Vega, W. A., & Gil, A. G. (2009). Substance abuse in minority populations. In Loue, S., & Sajatovic, M. (Eds.), Determinants of minority mental health and wellness (pp. 313-334). New York: Springer.

[2] French, K., Finkbiner, R., & Duhamel, L. (2002). Patterns of substance use among minority youth and adults in the United States: An overview and synthesis of national survey findings. Fairfax, VA: Caliber Associates.

[3] Vega. W. A., Aguilar-Gaxiola, S., Andrade, L., Bijl, R., Borges, G., Caraveo-Anduaga, J. J., DeWit, D. J., Heeringa, S. G., Kessler, R. C., Kolody, B., Merikangas, K. R., Molnar, B. E., Walters, E. E., Warner, L. A., & Wittchen, H. U. (2002). Prevalence and age of onset for drug use in seven international sites: Results from the International Consortium of Psychiatric Epidemiology. Drug and Alcohol Dependence, 68, 285-297.

[4] NSDUH asks a series of questions about race/ethnicity. First, respondents are asked about their Hispanic or Latino origin; then they are asked to identify which racial grouping best describes them: white, black or African American, American Indian or Alaska Native, Native Hawaiian, Other Pacific Islander, Asian, or other. Respondents may select more than one race. For this report, black or African American refers to persons identifying themselves as black or African American only. Persons identifying themselves as both black or African American and Hispanic or as both black or African American and another racial group are not included.

[5] NSDUH gathers data on family income, size, and composition (i.e., number of children) and respondent's age. This information is used to determine the respondent's poverty level. The poverty level is calculated as a percentage of the U.S. Census Bureau's poverty threshold by dividing the respondent's reported total family income by the appropriate poverty threshold amount. If a family's total income is less than the family's poverty threshold, then that family and every individual in it is considered to be living in poverty (i.e., less than 100 percent of the U.S. census poverty threshold). The poverty variable is available for the years from 2005 to 2009; therefore, information for this estimate is restricted to combined data from these years.

[6] Nonmedical use of prescription-type drugs is defined as the use of prescription-type drugs not prescribed for the respondent by a physician or used only for the experience or feeling they caused. Nonmedical use of any prescription-type pain reliever, sedative, stimulant, or

tranquilizer does not include over-the-counter drugs; nonmedical use of stimulants includes methamphetamine use.

In: Substance Use Among Select Ethnicities
Editor: Ron N. Gurovitz
ISBN: 978-1-62808-631-7


*Chapter 6*

# THE NSDUH REPORT: SUBSTANCE USE AMONG AMERICAN INDIAN AND ALASKA NATIVE ADOLESCENTS*

## *National Survey on Drug Use and Health*

## IN BRIEF

- Compared with the national average for adolescents aged 12 to 17, American Indian or Alaska Native adolescents had higher rates of past month cigarette use (16.8 vs. 10.2 percent), marijuana use (13.8 vs. 6.9 percent), and nonmedical use of prescription-type drugs (6.1 vs. 3.3 percent)
- The higher rates of substance use among American Indian or Alaska Native adolescents compared with national averages also were generally found among males, females, and across age groups
- Among adolescents aged 15 to 17, the rate of nonmedical use of prescription-type drugs in the past month among American Indians or Alaska Natives was higher than the national average (8.5 vs. 4.4 percent)

---

* This report (NSDUH 005) was released by the Substance Abuse and Mental Health Services Administration, Office of Applied Studies, October 4, 2011.

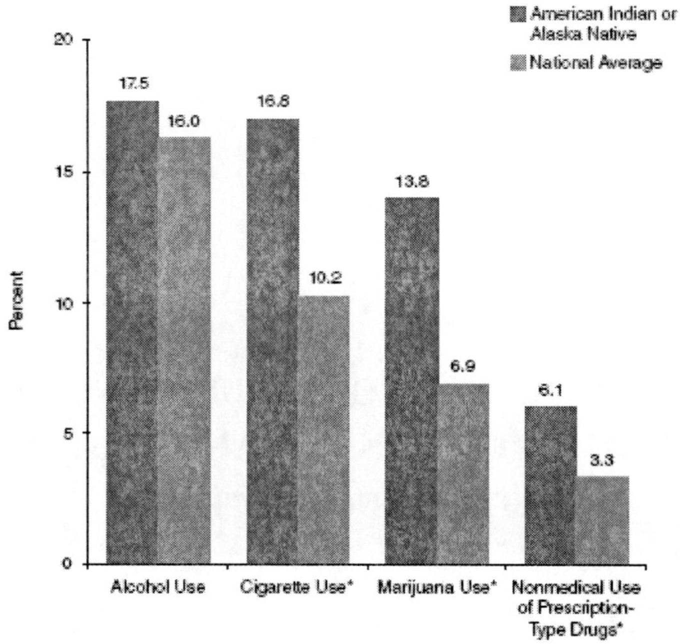


Source: 2004 to 2009 SAMHSA National Surveys on Drug Use and Health (NSDUHs).

* The difference between American Indian or Alaska Native adolescents and the national average is statistically significant at the .05 level.

Figure 1. Past Month Substance Use among American Indians or Alaska Natives Aged 12 to 17 Compared with the National Average: 2004 to 2009.

Although the American Indian or Alaska Native population is relatively small compared with other racial/ethnic groups in the United States, this population is disproportionately affected by a variety of health problems, including substance abuse.

Significant research has been aimed toward the American Indian or Alaska Native population by health providers and researchers to better understand and address their health needs. Particular interest has been focused on adolescents in an effort to help curb and prevent substance use among American Indian or Alaska Native youth. Monitoring substance use among American Indian or Alaska Native youth is important for informing prevention and treatment efforts and in reducing the substantial short- and long-term health, social, and economic costs that substance use imposes on these youth, and on their families and communities.[1]

This report examines substance use among non-Hispanic American Indian or Alaska Native adolescents (hereafter referred to as "American Indian or Alaska Native adolescents") aged 12 to 17, using combined data from the 2004 to 2009 National Surveys on Drug Use and Health (NSDUHs).[2] The report presented here is one in a series of reports intended to describe adolescent substance use within racial and ethnic subpopulations of the United States.

**Table 1. Past Month Substance Use among American Indians or Alaska Natives Aged 12 to 17 Compared with the National Average, by Age Group: 2004 to 2009**

| | Alcohol Use | | Cigarette Use | | Marijuana Use | | Nonmedical Use of Prescription-Type Drugs | |
|---|---|---|---|---|---|---|---|---|
| Age Group | American Indians or Alaska Natives (%) | National Average (%) | American Indians or Alaska Natives (%) | National Average (%) | American Indians or Alaska Natives (%) | National Average (%) | American Indians or Alaska Natives (%) | National Average (%) |
| Aged 12-14 | 10.2 | 6.2 | 7.7* | 3.5 | 5.6* | 2.0 | 3.8 | 2.0 |
| Aged 15-17 | 24.9 | 25.4 | 26.2* | 16.5 | 22.2* | 11.6 | 8.5* | 4.4 |

Source: 2004 to 2009 SAMHSA National Surveys on Drug Use and Health (NSDUHs).

* The difference between American Indian or Alaska Native adolescents and the national average is statistically significant at the .05 level.

## Demographic Characteristics

Combined 2004 to 2009 NSDUH data indicate that an annual average of about 150,000 persons aged 12 to 17—0.6 percent of the total population in this age group—identified themselves as non-Hispanic American Indian or Alaska Natives, with no other race reported.

American Indian or Alaska Native adolescents were similar to the national average in terms of age and gender distributions. Compared with the national average, however, American Indian or Alaska Native adolescents were twice as likely to be living in poverty3 (37.2 vs. 18.1 percent) and were more likely to live in non-metropolitan areas (50.1 vs. 16.5 percent).

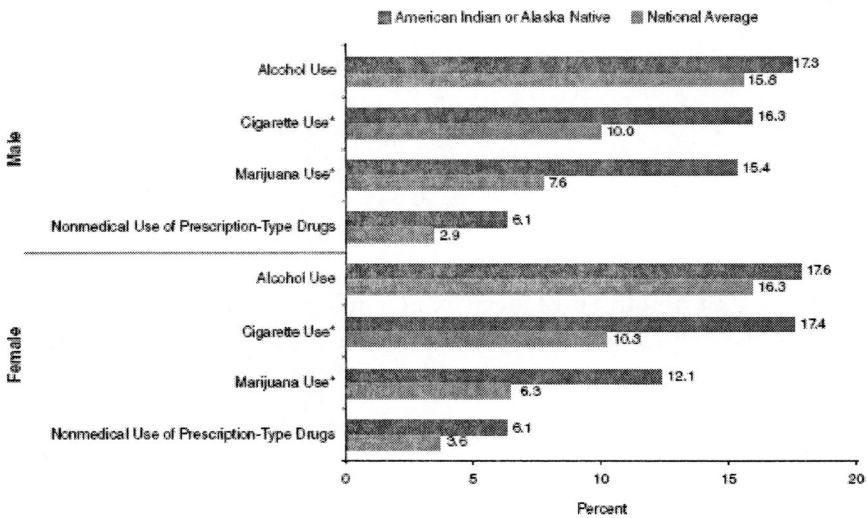


Source: 2004 to 2009 SAMHSA National Surveys on Drug Use and Health (NSDUHs).

* The difference between American Indian or Alaska Native adolescents and the national average is statistically significant at the .05 level.

Figure 2. Past Month Substance Use among American Indians or Alaska Natives Aged 12 to 17 Compared with the National Average, by Gender: 2004 to 2009.

## PAST MONTH SUBSTANCE USE

Substance use rates were generally higher among American Indian or Alaska Native adolescents compared with national averages (Figure 1).4 The greatest differences were found for cigarette use (16.8 vs. 10.2 percent) and marijuana use (13.8 vs. 6.9 percent). The rate of nonmedical use of prescription-type drugs among American Indian or Alaska Native adolescents was almost twice that of the national rate (6.1 vs. 3.3 percent). The rate of past month alcohol use among American Indian or Alaska Native youths was similar to the national rate.

## SUBSTANCE USE BY AGE GROUP

Compared with the national averages for 12 to 14 year olds, American Indians or Alaska Natives in this age group had higher rates of past month cigarette use (7.7 vs. 3.5 percent) and marijuana use (5.6 vs. 2.0 percent) (Table 1). Rates of past month alcohol use and nonmedical use of prescription-type drugs among American Indian or Alaska Native adolescents in this age group were not statistically different than those for same-aged adolescents in the Nation.

Compared with the national averages for 15 to 17 year olds, American Indians or Alaska Natives in this age group had higher rates of past month cigarette use (26.2 vs. 16.5 percent), marijuana use (22.2 vs. 11.6 percent), and nonmedical use of prescription-type drugs (8.5 vs. 4.4 percent). However, rates of past month alcohol use among American Indian or Alaska Native adolescents in this age group were similar to those for same-aged adolescents in the Nation as a whole.

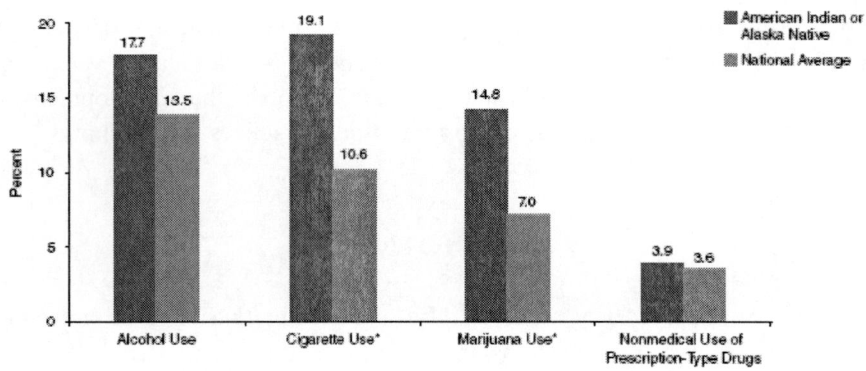


Source: 2005 to 2009 SAMHSA National Surveys on Drug Use and Health (NSDUHs).

* The difference between American Indian or Alaska Native adolescents and the national average is statistically significant at the .05 level.

Figure 3. Past Month Substance Use among American Indians or Alaska Natives Aged 12 to 17 Living in Poverty Compared with the National Average Living in Poverty: 2005 to 2009.

## SUBSTANCE USE AMONG ADOLESCENTS LIVING IN POVERTY

The rate of past month cigarette use among American Indian or Alaska Native adolescents living in poverty was higher than the national average for adolescents living in poverty (19.1 vs. 10.6 percent) as was the rate of past month use of marijuana (14.8 vs. 7.0 percent) (Figure 3). Rates of past month alcohol use and nonmedical use of prescription-type drugs did not differ significantly from the national averages for adolescents living in poverty.

## DISCUSSION

These data highlight the need for ongoing efforts to develop and implement behavioral health services for American Indian or Alaska Native adolescents. Furthermore, with 562 federally recognized tribal nations and Alaska Native villages where more than 200 tribal languages are spoken, prevention and treatment efforts aimed at American Indian or Alaska Native adolescents should be appropriately sensitive to the rich diversity of cultures among this popuation.[1] For example, effective prevention approaches may include those that incorporate American Indian or Alaska Native values, are provided in non-stigmatized settings, and involve the development of behavioral health systems that support traditional practices and teachings.[5]

## NOTE

The National Survey on Drug Use and Health (NSDUH) is an annual survey sponsored by the Substance Abuse and Mental Health Services Administration (SAMHSA). The 2004 to 2009 data used in this report are based on information obtained from 135,311 persons aged 12 to 17, including 1,907 American Indians or Alaska Natives. The survey collects data by administering questionnaires to a representative sample of the population through face-to-face interviews at their place of residence.

### End Notes

[1] Hawkins, E. H., Cummins, L. H., & Marlatt, G. A. (2004). Preventing substance abuse in American Indian and Alaska Native youth: Promising strategies for healthier communities. Psychological Bulletin, 130(2), 304-323.

[2] NSDUH asks a series of questions about race/ethnicity. First, respondents are asked about their Hispanic origin; then, they are asked to identify which racial grouping best describes them: White, Black or African American, American Indian or Alaska Native, Native Hawaiian, Other Pacific Islander, Asian, or other. Respondents may select more than one race. For this report, American Indian or Alaska Native refers to persons identifying themselves as

American Indian or Alaska Native only. Persons identifying as both American Indian or Alaska Native and Hispanic or as both American Indian or Alaska Native and another racial group are not included.

[3] NSDUH gathers data on family income, size, and composition (i.e., number of children) and respondent's age. This information is used to determine the respondent's poverty level. The poverty level is calculated as a percentage of the U.S. Census Bureau's poverty threshold by dividing the respondent's reported total family income by the appropriate poverty threshold amount. If a family's total income is less than the family's poverty threshold, then that family and every individual in it is considered to be living in poverty (i.e., less than 100 percent of the U.S. census poverty threshold). The poverty variable is available for the years from 2005 to 2009; therefore, information for this estimate is restricted to combined data from these years.

[4] Nonmedical use of prescription type drugs is defined as the use of prescription-type drugs not prescribed for the respondent by a physician or used only for the experience or feeling they caused. Nonmedical use of any prescription-type pain reliever, sedative, stimulant, or tranquilizer does not include over-the-counter drugs; nonmedical use of stimulants includes methamphetamine use.

[5] Goodkind, J. R., Ross-Toledo, K., John, S., Hall, J. L., Ross, L., Freeland, L., Coletta, E., Becenti-Fundark, T., Poola, C., Begay-Roanhorse, R., & Lee, C. (2010). Promoting healing and restoring trust: Policy recommendations for improving behavioral health care for American Indian/Alaska Native adolescents. American Journal of Community Psychology, 46, 386-394.

In: Substance Use Among Select Ethnicities ISBN: 978-1-62808-631-7
Editor: Ron N. Gurovitz 

*Chapter 7*

# THE NSDUH REPORT: SUBSTANCE USE AMONG HISPANIC ADOLESCENTS*

## *National Survey on Drug Use and Health*

## IN BRIEF

- Compared with the national average for adolescents aged 12 to 17, Hispanic adolescents had lower rates of past month cigarette use (8.1 vs. 10.2 percent), marijuana use (6.5 vs. 6.9 percent), and nonmedical use of prescription-type drugs (2.9 vs. 3.3 percent)
- Among Hispanic adolescents, marijuana use increased from 6.1 percent in 2008 to 8.1 percent in 2009, and remained steady at 8.0 percent in 2010; nonmedical use of prescription-type drugs increased from 2.2 percent in 2008 to 3.3 percent in 2009, and remained steady at 3.4 percent in 2010
- Among Hispanic adolescents, substance use varied by Hispanic subgroup; past month alcohol use, for example, ranged from 21.6 percent among Spanish adolescents to 13.8 percent among Puerto Rican adolescents

* This report (NSDUH 007) was released by the Substance Abuse and Mental Health Services Administration, Office of Applied Studies, October 4, 2011.

- Among Hispanic adolescents, those who were born in the United States had higher rates of past month cigarette use, alcohol use, and marijuana use than those who were not born in the United States

The Hispanic population in the United States grew by 15.2 million, or 43 percent, between 2000 and 2010, accounting for more than half of the total growth in the U.S. population in the last decade.[1] This level of growth is expected to continue into the foreseeable future, with particularly large increases projected in the Hispanic adolescent age group.[2] Furthermore, the Hispanic adolescent population consists of youth of different national origins with diverse cultural norms. As the Hispanic adolescent population continues to grow, it will become increasingly important to monitor substance use and other behavioral health problems among these youth as a whole and also by subgroups. Gaining a better understanding of substance use among Hispanic adolescents can help inform public health policy, build prevention and treatment programs that target the specific needs of these young people, and ultimately expand access to services for individuals who need them.

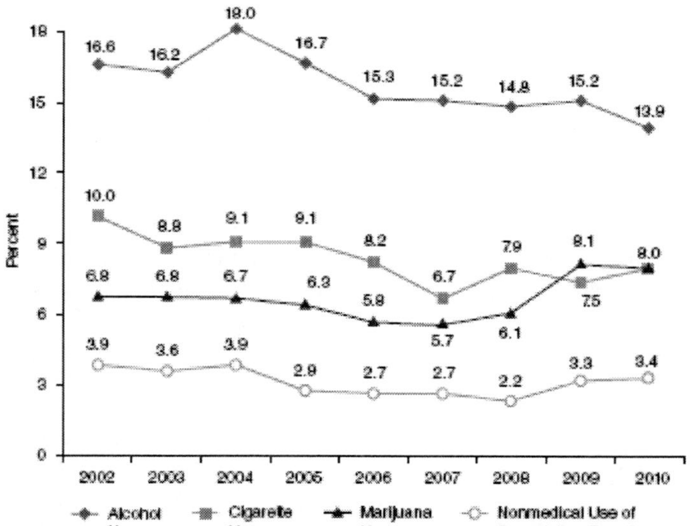


Source: 2002 to 2010 SAMHSA National Surveys on Drug Use and Health (NSDUHs).

Figure 1. Trends in Past Month Substance Use among Hispanics Aged 12 to 17: 2002 to 2010.

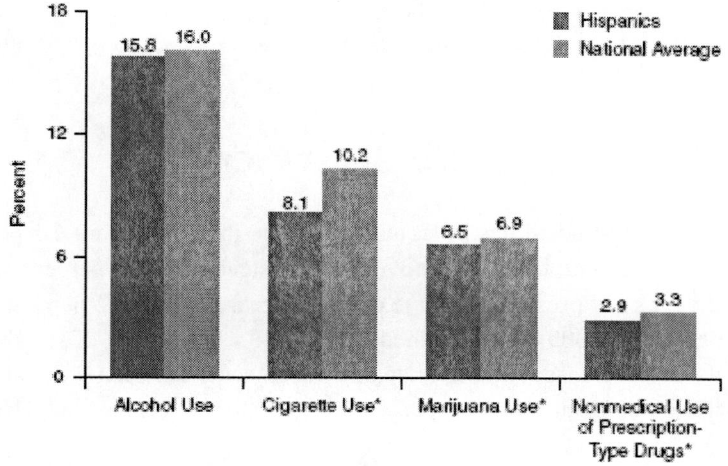


Source: 2004 to 2009 SAMHSA National Surveys on Drug Use and Health (NSDUHs).

* The difference between Hispanic adolescents and the national average is statistically significant at the .05 level.

Figure 2. Past Month Substance Use among Hispanics Aged 12 to 17 Compared with the National Average: 2004 to 2009.

This report examines substance use among Hispanic adolescents aged 12 to 17. Combined data from the 2004 to 2009 National Surveys on Drug Use and Health (NSDUHs) are used when discussing estimates, while the discussion on trends uses data from the 2002 to 2010 NSDUHs. The report presented here is one in a series of reports intended to describe adolescent substance use within racial and ethnic subpopulations of the United States.

## DEMOGRAPHIC CHARACTERISTICS

Combined 2004 to 2009 NSDUH data indicate that an annual average of 4.6 million persons aged 12 to 17—18.2 percent of the total population in this age group—identified themselves as Hispanic.[3] Two thirds (67.8 percent) of Hispanic adolescents were of Mexican origin, 10.2 percent were of Central or South American origin, and 10.0 percent were of Puerto Rican origin. The majority of Hispanic adolescents (81.8 percent) were born in the United States.[4] Compared with adolescents in the Nation as a whole, Hispanic adolescents were more likely to be living in poverty 5 (31.8 vs. 18.1 percent) and were less likely to have health insurance coverage (81.4 vs. 92.0 percent).

## Trends in Substance Use

Among Hispanic adolescents, marijuana use increased from 6.1 percent in 2008 to 8.1 percent in 2009, and remained steady at 8.0 percent in 2010; nonmedical use of prescription-type drugs6 increased from 2.2 percent in 2008 to 3.3 percent in 2009, and remained steady at 3.4 percent in 2010 (Figure 1). Cigarette use decreased among Hispanic adolescents between 2002 and 2010. Alcohol use declined from 16.6 percent in 2002 to 13.9 percent in 2010.

## Past Month Substance Use

Combined 2004 to 2009 data indicate that rates of past month substance use generally were lower among Hispanic adolescents compared with the national average for adolescents (Figure 2). The rate of past month cigarette use was lower among Hispanic adolescents than the national average for adolescents (8.1 vs. 10.2 percent).

Statistically significant differences were found for past month marijuana use (6.5 vs. 6.9 percent) and nonmedical use of prescriptiontype drugs (2.9 vs. 3.3 percent).

The rate of past month alcohol use among Hispanic adolescents was similar to the national average for adolescents.

## Substance Use by Hispanic Subgroup and Nativity

Among Hispanic adolescents, cigarette and alcohol use varied by Hispanic subgroup (Figure 3). Past month cigarette use ranged from 12.1 percent among adolescents of Spanish origin to 4.6 percent among adolescents of Dominican origin.

Past month alcohol use ranged from 21.6 percent among adolescents of Spanish origin to 13.8 percent among adolescents of Puerto Rican origin.

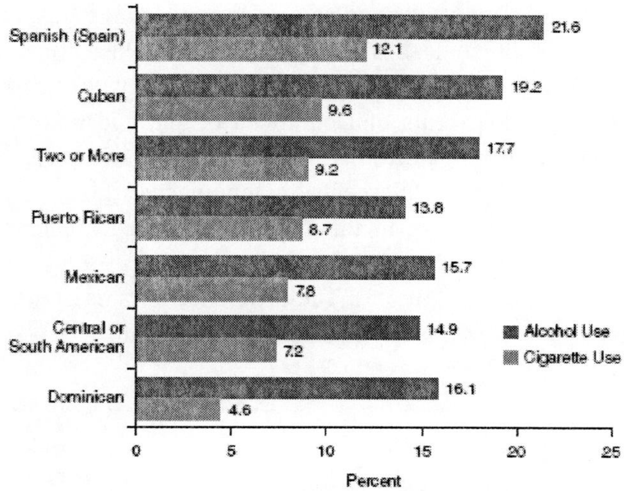


Source: 2004 to 2009 SAMHSA National Surveys on Drug Use and Health (NSDUHs).

Figure 3. Past Month Cigarette and Alcohol Use among Hispanics Aged 12 to 17, by Hispanic Subgroup: 2004 to 2009.

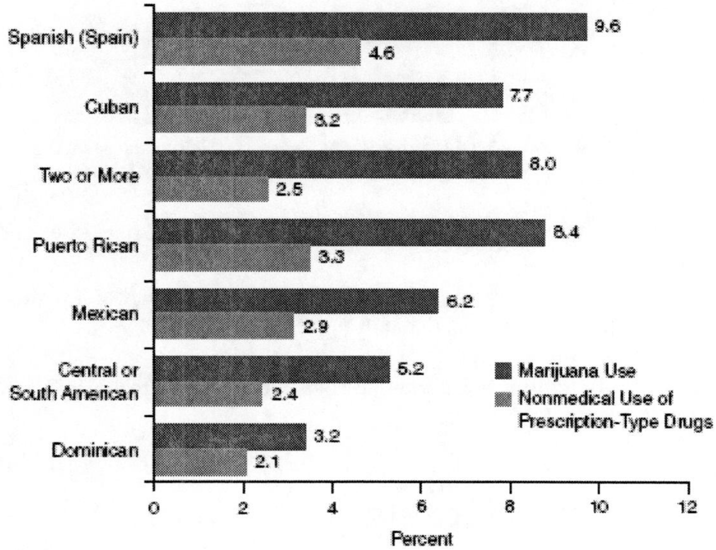


Source: 2004 to 2009 SAMHSA National Surveys on Drug Use and Health (NSDUHs).

Figure 4. Past Month Marijuana Use and Nonmedical Use of Prescription-Type Drugs among Hispanics Aged 12 to 17, by Hispanic Subgroup: 2004 to 2009.

Past month marijuana use varied across Hispanic subgroups, but there was little variation in nonmedical use of prescription-type drugs (Figure 4). Marijuana use ranged from 9.6 percent among adolescents of Spanish origin to 3.2 percent among adolescents of Dominican origin, and nonmedical use of prescription-type drugs ranged from 4.6 percent among adolescents of Spanish origin to 2.1 percent among adolescents of Dominican origin.

Hispanic adolescents born in the United States had higher rates of past month alcohol use, cigarette use, and marijuana use than those who were not born in the United States (Figure 5). The difference in rates of nonmedical use of prescription-type drugs was not statistically significant.

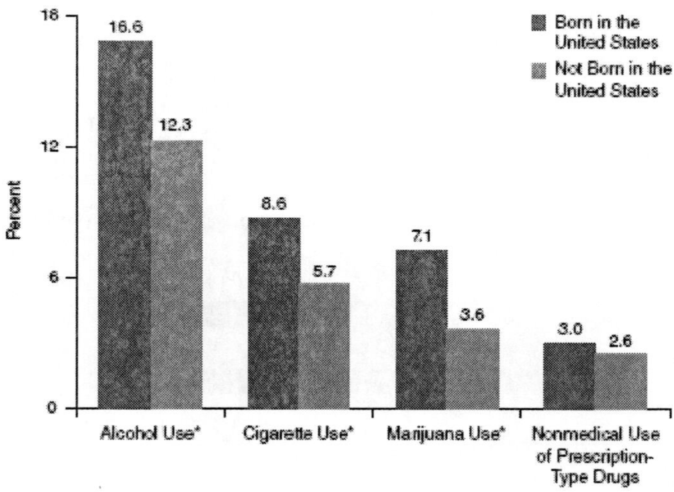


Source: 2004 to 2009 SAMHSA National Surveys on Drug Use and Health (NSDUHs).

* The difference between Hispanic adolescents born in the United States and those not born in the United States is statistically significant at the .05 level.

Figure 5. Past Month Substance Use among Hispanics Aged 12 to 17, by Nativity: 2004 to 2009.

## Substance Use by Age Group

For adolescents aged 12 to 14, there were statistically significant differences between rates for Hispanic youths and the national averages for youths for past month cigarette use and past month alcohol use, with cigarette use being slightly lower and alcohol use being slightly higher among Hispanics (Table 1).

Among adolescents aged 15 to 17, rates of past month cigarette use, marijuana use, and nonmedical use of prescription-type drugs among Hispanics were significantly lower than the national averages, while there was no statistically significant difference in rates of alcohol use.

## SUBSTANCE USE BY GENDER

Compared with the national averages for adolescent females, adolescent Hispanic females had lower rates of past month cigarette use and marijuana use (Figure 6).

Differences in rates of alcohol use and nonmedical use of prescription-type drugs were not statistically significant.

Adolescent Hispanic males had a lower rate of past month cigarette use than the national average for adolescent males; however, there were no statistically significant differences in rates for alcohol use, marijuana use, or nonmedical use of prescriptiontype drugs.

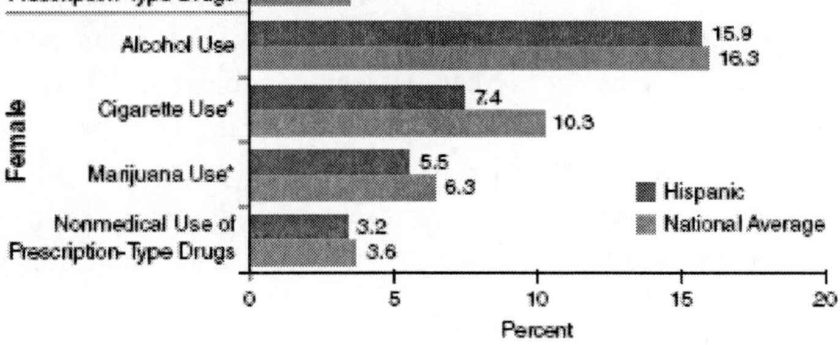


Source: 2004 to 2009 SAMHSA National Surveys on Drug Use and Health (NSDUHs).

* The difference between Hispanic adolescents and the national average is statistically significant at the .05 level.

**Table 1. Past Month Substance Use among Hispanics Aged 12 to 17 Compared with the National Average, by Age Group: 2004 to 2009**

| | Alcohol Use | | Cigarette Use | | Marijuana Use | | Nonmedical Use of Prescription-Type Drugs | |
|---|---|---|---|---|---|---|---|---|
| | Hispanics | National Average | Hispanics | National Average | Hispanics | National Average | Hispanics | National Average |
| Age Group | (%) | (%) | (%) | (%) | (%) | (%) | (%) | (%) |
| Aged 12-14 | 6.9* | 6.2 | 3.0* | 3.5 | 2.3 | 2.0 | 2.2 | 2.0 |
| Aged 15-17 | 24.9 | 25.4 | 13.3* | 16.5 | 10.7* | 11.6 | 3.7* | 4.4 |

Source: 2004 to 2009 SAMHSA National Surveys on Drug Use and Health (NSDUHs).

* The difference between Hispanic adolescents and the national average is statistically significant at the .05 level.

## DISCUSSION

Recent increases in rates of marijuana use and nonmedical use of prescription-type drugs among Hispanic adolescents suggest a need for prevention and treatment programs that target this population. Although substance use among Hispanic adolescents was generally lower than among adolescents in the Nation as a whole, certain subgroups of the Hispanic adolescent population had rates of use that exceeded the rates in the general population, and Hispanic adolescents born in the United States were more likely to use illicit substances than Hispanic adolescents born elsewhere. While Hispanic adolescents had lower prevalence rates than national averages for certain substances, prevention and treatment strategies targeting this population need to account for the variations by age, gender, and nativity to help assist Hispanic adolescents maintain or achieve a healthier lifestyle.

## NOTE

The National Survey on Drug Use and Health (NSDUH) is an annual survey sponsored by the Substance Abuse and Mental Health Services

Administration (SAMHSA). The 2004 to 2009 data used in this report are based on information obtained from 135,311 persons aged 12 to 17, including 22,195 Hispanics.

The survey collects data by administering questionnaires to a representative sample of the population through face-to-face interviews at their place of residence.

## END NOTES

[1] Humes, K. R., Jones, N. A., & Ramirez, R. R. (2010, March). Overview of race and Hispanic origin: 2010. (2010 Census Briefs, C2010BR-02). Suitland, MD: U.S. Census Bureau. Retrieved from: http://www. census.gov/prod/cen2010/briefs/c2010br-02.pdf.

[2] Numbers were calculated from various census tables: U.S. Census Bureau. (2010, September 16). National characteristics. Retrieved from http:// www.census.gov/population/www/ projections/usinterimproj/

[3] NSDUH asks a series of questions about race/ethnicity. First, respondents are asked about their Hispanic origin; then they are asked to identify which racial grouping best describes them: white, black/African American, American Indian or Alaska Native, Native Hawaiian, other Pacific Islander, Asian, or other. Respondents may select more than one race. For this report, respondents identifying themselves as Hispanic were assigned to the Hispanic group regardless of their racial identification. Individuals who identify themselves as Hispanic are asked to name a Hispanic subgroup that best describes them; response options include Mexican/Mexican American/Mexicano/Chicano, Puerto Rican, Central or South American, Cuban/Cuban American, Dominican (from the Dominican Republic), Spanish (from Spain), and other. Respondents may select more than one Hispanic subgroup.

[4] Respondents were asked if they were born in the United States, and responses to this question were used to differentiate U.S.-born versus foreign-born Hispanics. All findings in the report pertain strictly to residents of the United States, not to persons living in other countries. No information is collected on citizenship; thus, no inferences can be made in this regard.

[5] NSDUH gathers data on family income, size, and composition (i.e., number of children) and respondent's age. This information is used to determine the respondent's poverty level. The poverty level is calculated as a percentage of the U.S. Census Bureau's poverty threshold by dividing the respondent's reported total family income by the appropriate poverty threshold amount. If a family's total income is less than the family's poverty threshold, then that family and every individual in it is considered to be living in poverty (i.e., less than 100 percent of the U.S. census poverty threshold). The poverty variable is available for the years from 2005 to 2009; therefore, information for this estimate is restricted to combined data from these years.

[6] Nonmedical use of prescription-type drugs is defined as the use of prescription-type drugs not prescribed for the respondent by a physician or used only for the experience or feeling they caused. Nonmedical use of any prescription-type pain reliever, sedative, stimulant, or tranquilizer does not include over-the-counter drugs; nonmedical use of stimulants includes methamphetamine use.

In: Substance Use Among Select Ethnicities
Editor: Ron N. Gurovitz
ISBN: 978-1-62808-631-7


*Chapter 8*

# THE NSDUH REPORT: SUBSTANCE USE AMONG ASIAN ADOLESCENTS*

## *National Survey on Drug Use and Health*

## IN BRIEF

- Asian adolescents aged 12 to 17 had lower rates compared with the national average of past month cigarette use (3.9 vs. 10.2 percent), alcohol use (7.4 vs. 16.0 percent), marijuana use (2.9 vs. 6.9 percent), and nonmedical use of prescription-type drugs (1.8 vs. 3.3 percent)
- Among Asian adolescents, substance use varied by Asian subgroup; past month alcohol use, for example, ranged from a high of 9.7 percent among Filipino adolescents to a low of 5.1 percent among Asian Indian adolescents
- Asian adolescents who were born in the United States had a higher rate of past month alcohol use than Asian adolescents who were not born in the United States (8.7 vs. 4.7 percent), while the rate of nonmedical use of prescription-type drugs was higher among Asian adolescents not born in the United States than among those born in the United States (2.7 vs. 1.4 percent)

* This report (NSDUH 006) was released by the Substance Abuse and Mental Health Services Administration, Office of Applied Studies, October 4, 2011.

According to the U.S. Census Bureau, the Asian adolescent population is projected to increase by 50 percent between 2011 and 2050 (1.0 vs. 2.2 million), making them one of the fastest-growing segments of the adolescent population in the United States.[1] Furthermore, the Asian-American adolescent population consists of many different ethnic subgroups, each having its own cultural norms. As the Asian adolescent population grows, monitoring substance use and other behavioral health problems among these youth as a whole and also by ethnic subgroup becomes increasingly important. Gaining a better understanding of substance use among Asian adolescents can help inform public health policy, build prevention and treatment programs that target the specific needs of these young people, and ultimately expand access to services.

This report uses data from the National Survey on Drug Use and Health (NSDUH) to examine substance use among non-Hispanic Asian adolescents (hereafter referred to as "Asian adolescents") between the ages of 12 and 17.[2] Findings in the report are annual averages based on combined 2004 to 2009 NSDUH data.

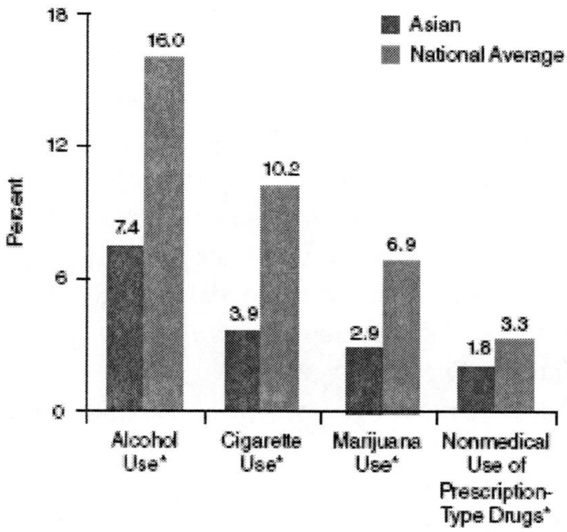


Source: 2004 to 2009 SAMHSA National Surveys on Drug Use and Health (NSDUHs).

* The difference between Asian adolescents and the national average is statistically significant at the .05 level.

Figure 1. Past Month Substance Use among Asians Aged 12 to 17 Compared with the National Average: 2004 to 2009.

## DEMOGRAPHIC CHARACTERISTICS

Combined 2004 to 2009 NSDUH data indicate that an annual average of 1.0 million persons aged 12 to 17—4.0 percent of the total population in this age—identified themselves as Asian. About one quarter (24.2 percent) of Asian adolescents reported being Asian Indian, 19.8 percent were Chinese, 16.8 percent were Filipino, 10.7 percent were Korean, 9.9 percent were Vietnamese, 3.7 percent were Japanese, and 15.0 percent were from other Asian subgroups. About two thirds (66.7 percent) of Asian adolescents were born in the United States.[3] Asian adolescents were similar to the national average in terms of age and gender distributions, as well as the percentage living in poverty.[4] Asian adolescents were more likely to live in large metropolitan areas than the national average of adolescents (75.7 vs. 53.5 percent) and less likely to live in non-metropolitan areas (3.1 vs. 16.5 percent).

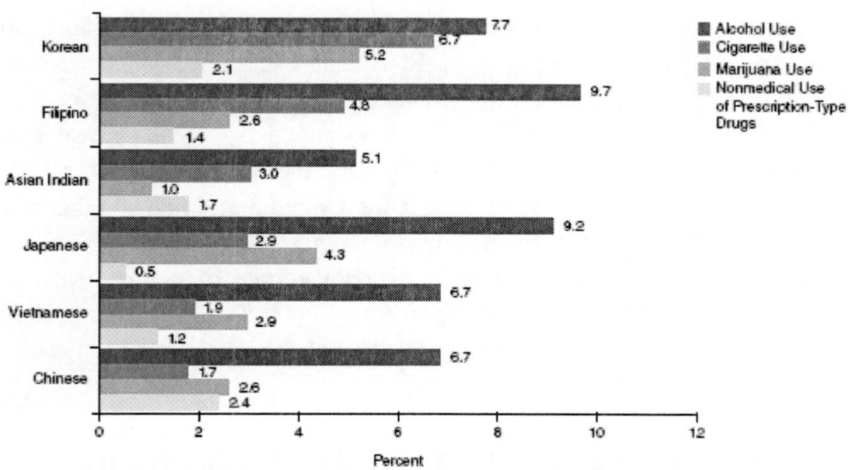


Source: 2004 to 2009 SAMHSA National Surveys on Drug Use and Health (NSDUHs).

Figure 2. Past Month Substance Use among Asians Aged 12 to 17, by Subgroup: 2004 to 2009.

## PAST MONTH SUBSTANCE USE

Rates of past month substance use were lower among Asian adolescents compared with national averages (Figure 1). For example, the rate of alcohol use among Asian adolescents was about half that of the national rate (7.4 vs. 16.0 percent). Cigarette use (3.9 vs. 10.2 percent) and marijuana use (2.9 vs. 6.9 percent) followed a similar pattern. The rate of nonmedical use of prescription-type drugs[5] also was lower among Asian adolescents than the national average for adolescents (1.8 vs. 3.3 percent).

## SUBSTANCE USE BY ASIAN SUBGROUP AND NATIVITY

Among Asian adolescents, past month cigarette and alcohol use varied by Asian subgroup (Figure 2). For example, past month cigarette use ranged from a high of 6.7 percent among Korean adolescents to a low of 1.7 percent among Chinese adolescents. Past month alcohol use ranged from a high of 9.7 percent among Filipino adolescents to a low of 5.1 percent among Asian Indian adolescents.

Past month marijuana use and nonmedical use of prescription-type drugs also varied across Asian subgroups. Marijuana use ranged from 5.2 percent among Korean adolescents to 1.0 percent among Asian Indian adolescents, and nonmedical use of prescription-type drugs ranged from 2.4 percent among Chinese adolescents to 0.5 percent among Japanese adolescents.

Asian adolescents who were born in the United States had a higher rate of past month alcohol use than Asian adolescents who were not born in the United States (8.7 vs. 4.7 percent) and a lower rate of nonmedical use of prescription-type drugs (1.4 vs. 2.7 percent) (Figure 3). Rates of cigarette use and marijuana use did not differ significantly between these two groups.

## SUBSTANCE USE BY AGE GROUP AND GENDER

For adolescents aged 12 to 14 and 15 to 17, rates of past month cigarette use, alcohol use, and marijuana use among Asians were lower than national averages (Table 1). Among adolescents aged 15 to 17, the rate of past month nonmedical use of prescription-type drugs among Asians was lower than the national average (2.0 vs. 4.4 percent), but the difference for those aged 12 to 14 was not statistically significant.

For both genders, rates of past month alcohol use, cigarette use, marijuana use, and nonmedical use of prescription-type drugs were lower among Asian adolescents than among adolescents in the Nation as a whole (Figure 4).

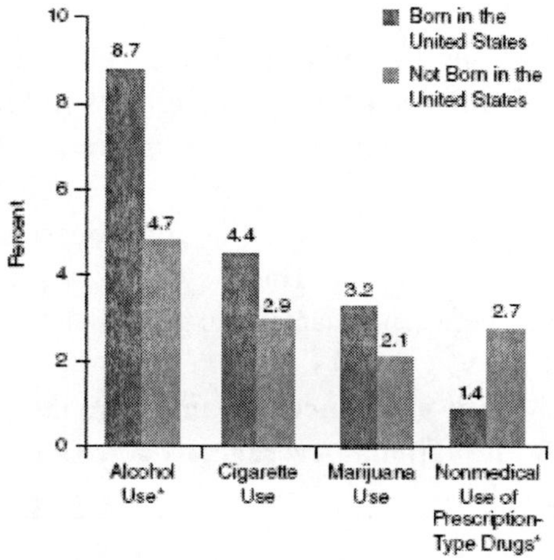


Source: 2004 to 2009 SAMHSA National Surveys on Drug Use and Health (NSDUHs).

* The difference between Asian adolescents born in the United States and those not born in the United States is statistically significant at the .05 level.

Figure 3. Past Month Substance Use among Asians Aged 12 to 17, by Nativity: 2004 to 2009.

## SUBSTANCE USE AMONG ADOLESCENTS LIVING IN POVERTY

The rates of past month alcohol use, cigarette use, and marijuana use among Asian adolescents living in poverty were lower than the national averages for adolescents living in poverty (Figure 5). The rate of nonmedical use of prescription-type drugs among Asian adolescents living in poverty was not statistically different from the national average for adolescents living in poverty.

## DISCUSSION

The data in this report show that certain segments of the Asian population may be at greater risk for substance use than others. For example, the rate of past month cigarette use among Korean adolescents was 3 times higher than among Chinese or Vietnamese adolescents. Although Asian adolescents generally had lower rates of substance use than adolescents in the Nation as a whole, these data highlight the importance of monitoring substance use data among the diverse populations of Asian adolescents in the United States and being cognizant not only of gender and age differences but also of cultural differences. The data also suggest specific subgroups within the Asian adolescent community that may benefit from increased attention from prevention and treatment systems. These systems will need to account for differences among and between Asian ethnic groups and level of acculturation.

**Table 1. Past Month Substance Use among Asians Aged 12 to 17 Compared with the National Average, by Age Group: 2004 to 2009**

| | Alcohol Use | | Cigarette Use | | Marijuana Use | | Nonmedical Use of Prescription-Type Drugs | |
|---|---|---|---|---|---|---|---|---|
| | Asians | National Average | Asians | National Average | Asians | National Average | Asians | National Average |
| Age Group | (%) | (%) | (%) | (%) | (%) | (%) | (%) | (%) |
| Aged 12-14 | 2.7* | 6.2 | 0.8* | 3.5 | 0.5* | 2.0 | 1.6 | 2.0 |
| Aged 15-17 | 11.5* | 25.4 | 6.6* | 16.5 | 4.9* | 11.6 | 2.0* | 4.4 |

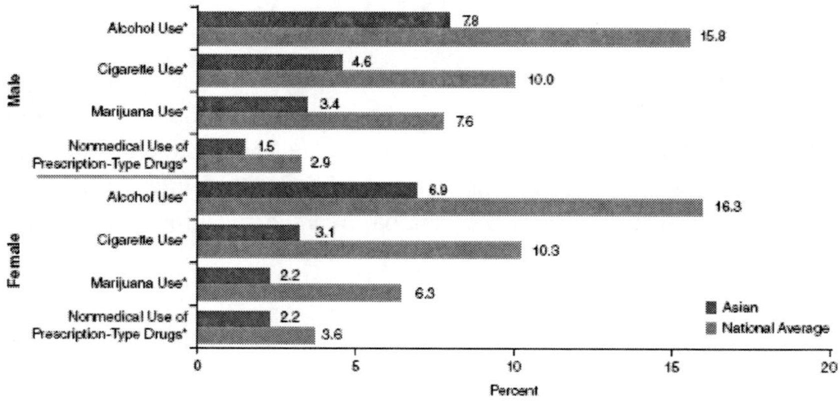


* The difference between Asian adolescents and the national average is statistically significant at the .05 level. Source: 2004 to 2009 SAMHSA National Surveys on Drug Use and Health (NSDUHs).

Figure 4. Past Month Substance Use among Asians Aged 12 to 17 Compared with the National Average, by Gender: 2004 to 2009.

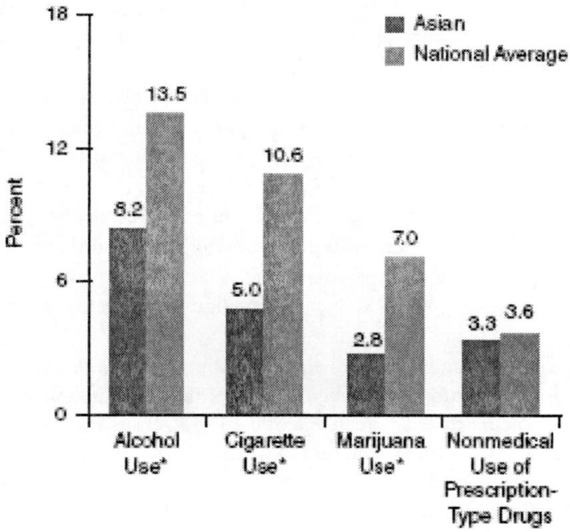


* The difference between Asian adolescents and the national average is statistically significant at the .05 level.

Source: 2005 to 2009 SAMHSA National Surveys on Drug Use and Health (NSDUHs).

Figure 5. Past Month Substance Use among Asians Aged 12 to 17 Living in Poverty Compared with the National Average Living in Poverty: 2005 to 2009.

# NOTE

The National Survey on Drug Use and Health (NSDUH) is an annual survey sponsored by the Substance Abuse and Mental Health Services Administration (SAMHSA). The 2004 to 2009 data used in this report are based on information obtained from 135,311 persons aged 12 to 17, including 3,763 Asian adolescents. The survey collects data by administering questionnaires to a representative sample of the population through face-to-face interviews at their place of residence.

## End Notes

[1] U.S. Census Bureau. (2010, September 16). National characteristics. Retrieved from http://www.census.gov/population/www/projections/ usinterimproj/

[2] NSDUH asks a series of questions about race/ethnicity. First, respondents are asked about their Hispanic origin; then they are asked to identify which racial grouping(s) best describes

them: white, black or African American, American Indian, Alaska Native, Native Hawaiian, Other Pacific Islander, Asian, or other. Individuals who identify themselves as Asian also are asked to name an Asian subgroup that best describes them; response options include Asian Indian, Chinese, Filipino, Japanese, Korean, Vietnamese, and other. Respondents may select more than one race. For this report, "Asian" refers to persons identifying themselves as Asian only. Persons identifying as Asian and Hispanic or Asian and another racial group are not included.

[3] Respondents were asked if they were born in the United States, and responses to this question were used to differentiate Asians born in the United States and those not born in the United States. All findings in the report pertain strictly to residents of the United States, not to persons living in other countries. No information is collected on citizenship; thus, no inferences can be made in this regard.

[4] NSDUH gathers data on family income, size, and composition (i.e., number of children) and respondent's age. This information is used to determine the respondent's poverty level. The poverty level is calculated as a percentage of the U.S. Census Bureau's poverty threshold by dividing the respondent's reported total family income by the appropriate poverty threshold amount. If a family's total income is less than the family's poverty threshold, then that family and every individual in it is considered to be living in poverty (i.e., less than 100 percent of the U.S. census poverty threshold). The poverty variable is available for the years from 2005 to 2009; therefore, information for this estimate is restricted to combined data from these years.

[5] Nonmedical use of prescription-type drugs is defined as the use of prescription-type drugs not prescribed for the respondent by a physician or used only for the experience or feeling they caused. Nonmedical use of any prescription-type pain reliever, sedative, stimulant, or tranquilizer does not include over-the-counter drugs; nonmedical use of stimulants includes methamphetamine use.

# INDEX

## D



## E



## F



## G



## H



## I



## L



## M

## W



## Y